D0366192

CONTENTS

Introduction

The traditional division of labor with men installing shelves and grateful women cleaning up the mess now seems quaint as well as politically incorrect.

Nowadays it is not unusual for women to be able to cook a meal for four, check the children's homework, download the latest music to our MP3 player, and program the DVD recorder while also holding down a responsible full-time job. And if that's not enough, many are taking on home-improvement chores. However, their upbringing did not usually include how to wield a hammer, saw, and drill, which is why *The Little Book of Tips and Quick Fixes for the Home Handywoman* is so useful (for some men, too). Packed full of essential tips, useful facts, and the quickest of quick fixes, it guides you through the basic home-improvement jobs that you're likely to want to attempt. And by learning what's hidden behind your walls and under your floors, and the kinds of problems that can arise when you "do it yourself," you'll be able to judge whether to try to do the job yourself or leave it to the experts.

This little book offers you common-sense tips ranging from how to choose the essential tools, through learning basic skills and dealing with plumbing and electricity, right through to making simple furniture without resorting to the gin bottle. And if you also missed out on learning the art of housework, there's even advice on how to keep your newly revamped home spick-and-span!

So buy yourself a set of spanking new tools and get down to business.

Bridget Bodoano

THE TOOLS

Handywoman helpline

Q: I'm a total novice when it comes to do-it-yourself home improvements but I'd like to get started. The problem is, I'm completely stumped when it comes to deciding how much to spend on my tools. There's such a wide range of prices. Can you help?

A: For items such as basic hand tools, the price will reflect the quality. For a beginner, though, inexpensive tools are usually perfectly adequate. For anything that involves machinery, motors, or electricity, it's better to go for a reputable, well-known brand. Then you can be sure that what you buy will conform to the necessary standards and safety regulations.

Ten tool tips

1 Treat yourself to a smart box or bag with compartments or pockets to store your tools.

2 Make sure your toolbox is easily accessible.

3 Always put tools back in their box or bag once you have finished with them.

4 Keep any instructions for use with the tools.

5 Buy a power drill that comes in a handy bag with storage for all its attachments.

Keep all sharp blades covered when not in use.

Carefully throw away all old disposable blades.

Always keep a pair of rubber gloves, safety goggles, a dust mask, and some bandaids in your toolbox.

Keep screwdriver sets and wrenches together in their original packaging or in a pocketed cloth roll.

For a safe and comfortable grip, always choose power tools that fit your hand size and are not too heavy.

Do your homework

The range of tools on offer in most home-improvement stores is large, but information is scarce, so do a little research before you shop. Browsing through catalogs and looking on the internet is a good way to discover the function and power of different products. Many companies have a helpline that dispenses good advice—and don't worry if you sound like a novice.

What do I need?

There's a huge number of frightening-looking tools on the market, but most basic do-it-yourself jobs can be done with a select few.

BRADAWL: A short, sharp spike on a chunky handle. Used for marking the position of and making pilot holes (see page 33).

UTILITY KNIFE: With a chunky, easy-to-grip handle with a strong replaceable blade, a utility knife is used for cutting everything from cardboard to carpet.

CARPENTER'S LEVEL: A device that shows whether surfaces and edges are plumb. Essential for installing shelves.

CLAW HAMMER: Needed for knocking in nails, but more frequently for taking them out. Also invaluable for minor demolition work.

TAPE MEASURE: For measuring rooms or marking smaller distances. A medium-width 10-foot-long tape measure will fit nicely in your hand.

FRAMING SQUARE: Useful for marking lengths of wood and cutting and checking right angles.

SCREWDRIVERS: A slotted-head screwdriver has a flat point and is used for screws with a straight slot in the head. A cross-head screwdriver is used for screws with a cross-shaped slot. You'll need both in various sizes and lengths. Power screwdrivers are easier, faster, and screw tighter—and in reverse gear they're great for undoing screws.

WRENCHES: For tightening and undoing nuts and bolts. Adjustable wrenches can be altered to fit any size bolt but are a little unwieldy.

PLIERS: For gripping objects so you can turn, squeeze, pinch or pull out a variety of things, from nails in awkward corners to screw tops that won't unscrew. Some can cut wire, too. Blunt-nose pliers are good for general use but the long-nose variety are useful for more precise work.

SAWS: Buy an all-purpose saw for cutting wood, metal, and plastics. Also invest in a small hacksaw with a thin, replaceable blade, which is useful for cutting metal and plastic pipes.

Resist temptation

There are several tempting-looking power tools on the market but to start with, resist buying anything other than a power drill. Power planers, circular saws, and belt sanders need a higher level of skill and can always be rented if necessary.

All power to your elbow

Drill power is expressed in volts: the higher the voltage the more powerful and versatile the tool. Power drills/drivers, for example, usually range from about 9.6V to 36V.

Five things to look for when buying a power drill/driver

1 **POWER:** If you want to drill into masonry, check the drill specifications to make sure it is powerful enough.

2 **VARIABLE SPEED:** Speed is given in revs per minute (rpm). Most general-purpose drills go up to 3000 rpm. You need a lower speed for drilling into particularly hard surfaces, and a faster speed for wood, to give a neat finish and prevent splitting. A slow speed is also necessary to use the power driver as a screwdriver.

3 **REVERSE:** Reverse is essential if you're going to use the driver to remove as well as drive in screws. It also comes in handy if the drill bit gets stuck.

HAMMER OR PERCUSSION ACTION: This is necessary for drilling in masonry.

 ATTACHMENTS: Often a range of accessories can be added for sanding and polishing. You never know when they may come in handy.

Corded versus cordless

Cordless tools were developed for use in places where being attached to a power cord can be difficult or dangerous, such as outside or up a tall ladder. While cord-free drilling is convenient, there are disadvantages. For example, the power isn't consistent—it will lessen as the battery runs down—and you may not always remember to recharge the battery. Buy a spare and keep it charged so it's ready for use when the first battery goes flat.

If you're using a corded tool, it can be just as convenient but always be aware of the power cord. Don't get entangled in it and, if it's too short to allow free movement, use an extension cord.

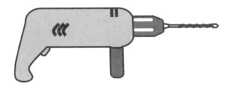

"Buy a spare and keep it
charged so it's ready for use
when the first battery goes flat."

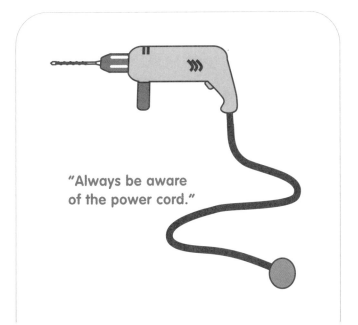

"Always be aware
of the power cord."

DRILLING A HOLE

About drill bits

The part of the drill that actually makes the hole is called the bit. Bits come in a variety of shapes and sizes suited to different functions and materials. They're sized in fractional incehs and each one is ascribed a number or letter gauge size.

✳ **A MASONRY BIT** has a tungsten-carbide tip and is used for plaster, concrete, and brick.

✳ **A WOOD BIT** has a sharp cutting thread and a point for accurate positioning.

✳ **A METAL BIT** is made from hard steel and has a V-shaped tip. As well as being used for cutting metal, it can also be used for wood.

✳ **A COUNTERSINK BIT** has a short, wide pointed end. It drills a shallow cone-shaped recess in wood for countersinking screws—so that when the screw is in place, its head is flush with, or below the surface of the wood. The recess can then be filled with wood filler to give a smooth surface.

✳ **A FLAT WOOD BIT** has a central point and flat steel on each side. It is used to drill a fairly large hole in wood.

Drilling drill

Before drilling into any wall, floor, or ceiling you must check if there's an electricity cable or a gas or water pipe so you can avoid making a hole in it. So don't drill near electrical outlets or immediately above, below, or around switches or light fixtures.

You can buy inexpensive, battery-powered devices that light up to indicate the presence of metal pipes in walls or under floors, or to detect the position of electrical cables.

How deep, how wide?

The depth and diameter of the hole you need to drill will depend on the size of the screw and, if you are using one, the length of the anchor plug (see page 67). To ensure that the hole is the right length, wrap a piece of tape around the drill bit to mark the depth required or use the adjustable depth stop sometimes supplied with a power drill.

Remember that a certain amount of dust and debris will collect at the far end of the hole as you drill, so you need to drill a little deeper than the length of the anchor plug.

Handywoman helpline

Q: It's sometimes difficult to drive a screw into a piece of wood. Can you suggest any tips?

A: A screw will go into wood more easily and more accurately if there's a pilot hole to start if off. You can make one using a bradawl or a drill with a fine bit. Similarly, if you are putting up hooks or eyes with a screw thread, they'll also be easier to screw in with a pilot hole.

Nails don't ordinarily need a drilled hole but if they're very long or the wood is very thick, they'll also benefit from a pilot hole. This will reduce the risk of the nail bending, going in at the wrong angle, or splitting the wood.

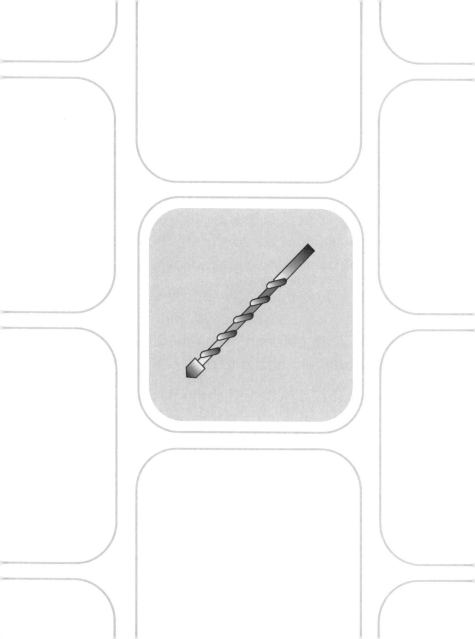

The drill for special surfaces

✳ To avoid cracking or chipping ceramic tiles when you drill them, stick a piece of masking tape on top of the tile to help position the drill bit and stop it from slithering and shooting off across the tile. Use a masonry bit but set the drill to rotary action and use a slow speed.

✳ When drilling into fairly soft metal, make a small dent with a nail set or a bradawl and place the V-shaped end of the metal bit into this dent before starting to drill.

✳ Always drill downward through the top of plastic-coated laminated plank flooring. Drilling upward from below can crack it.

Drilling a hole in a wall

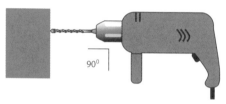

1 Check that there are no wires or pipes in the wall. Mark the center of the hole. Place the point of the drill bit firmly on this mark at a 90-degree angle to the wall.

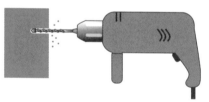

2 Turn on the drill. Keeping it as level and straight as possible, push the drill bit gently into the wall. Continue pushing until the hole is drilled to the depth required.

3 Insert an anchor plug (see page 67) into the drilled hole and tap it gently into place with a hammer.

4 To secure your fixture (such as a coat hook), place it against the wall so that the screw hole and drilled hole line up, insert the screw, hold firmly in place, and tighten with a screwdriver.

Drilling a hole for a pipe

1 Mark the cutting lines on each side of the pipe.

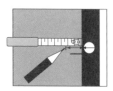

2 Measure the distance from the wall to the front of the pipe and mark this distance on the shelf/worktop.

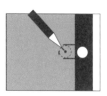

3 Mark the center of the hole to be drilled. This is where you position the drill bit.

4 Drill out the hole using a power drill fitted with a flat wood bit.

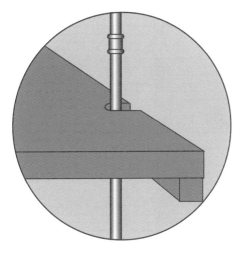

5 Cut along the marked lines using a saw, then position the cut surface around the pipe.

SAWING & CUTTING

Get a grip

It helps to have a simple workbench with clamps or a vise to hold the piece you're cutting between two lengths of wood. The workbench also gives you a level surface to work on and the clamps can also be used to hold things you're drilling or sanding.

"Measure twice, cut once." Whatever you're cutting, make this your mantra.

Handywoman helpline

Q: I can never seem to manage to use a handsaw properly. Are there any special tips I should bear in mind?

A: Start by placing the blade of the saw on the marked spot on the edge of the wood. Then dig the blade gently into the wood and draw it backward a little way to cut a small nick. Using the nick to locate the saw blade—and making sure that it's vertical and lined up with the cutting line—start sawing by pushing the blade forward and pulling it backward, always cutting down at an angle of 90 degrees.

HANDYWOMAN SAWING TIP

To begin with, you may find that the saw sticks and you have to keep restarting, but once you get into a regular rhythm, try not to stop until you have cut right through.

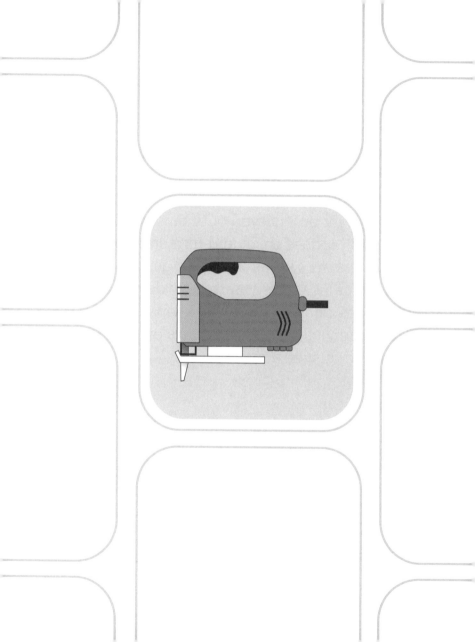

Power jigsaws

A power jigsaw isn't that difficult to use and will give a neater, straighter cut than a handsaw, and with a lot less effort. Most will make straight and curved cuts in wood up to about 2¾ inches thick and in metal up to ¼ inch thick, as well as in most plastics. Variable speed allows you to slow down for tricky areas and a dustblower keeps the cutting line visible—some models even extract the dust as you saw.

A professional cut

For large pieces of wood and long cuts, it sometimes pays to have a professional do the job. Many home-improvement stores will cut wood (straight cuts only) to your precise measurements. The service can be free or carry only a small charge.

Before you go shopping, check the dimensions of standard lengths and widths of lumber so you can work out the most economical way of buying what you need. Draw diagrams of your requirements and mark the measurements.

Once you have bought the wood you need, load it on your cart and take it, along with your diagrams, to the cutting-service area. Sometimes these services are much in demand so don't ask for too much to be cut at one time. Or try to go at less busy times.

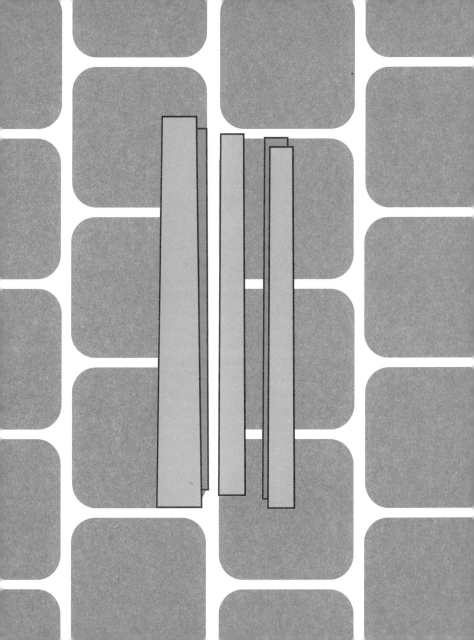

Cutting plastics

Plastic edging and pipes are easy enough to cut, but sheets are more troublesome. Soft plastic can clog the teeth of the saw and thicker, harder materials, such as acrylic sheets, will crack unless cut carefully. Acrylics are also expensive, so it's best to have them cut and finished professionally.

Cutting tiles

A tile cutter (see page 136) will make clean straight cuts in ceramic tiles, but for awkward shapes you'll need to use tile nippers (see page 136). These require care and a certain amount of skill.

Cutting wires and cables

Some pliers have a cutting blade that cuts electrical wires and cables, and some have a notch for stripping off the plastic sheath.

Light cuts...

Utility knives can be used for wallpaper, carpet, vinyl, and thin plastic. Those with replaceable blades are versatile since you can get a variety of blades such as a small saw blade and a curved blade for cutting carpet.

...and heavy cuts

For cutting through thick metal, ceramic, or stone, you'll need to resort to a specialty power tool. It has a tough, circular blade that whizzes around really fast. Although it isn't expensive and looks small and manageable, the effort needed and the noise and dust it generates during use means it's more suited to builders than beginners.

Metal special

✳ Cutting metal is easier than it sounds but to begin with it's best to avoid cutting sheet metal or heavy metal fittings or fixtures.

✳ Metal tubes are frequently used for curtain rods, clothes-hanging rails, and plumbing. To cut them, use a small hacksaw with a thin, replaceable blade. This works but it can be difficult to control because the blade is flexible.

✳ Alternatively, use a pipe cutter. This is an ingenious device that holds the pipe in place while a small blade, tightened by a hand-turned screw, makes a neat, straight cut.

✳ Cutting metal produces a lot of heat, so don't touch the edges of the metal or the saw until things have cooled down.

✳ Smooth off ragged edges with a file or abrasive paper but be careful not to cut your fingers on any sharp metal.

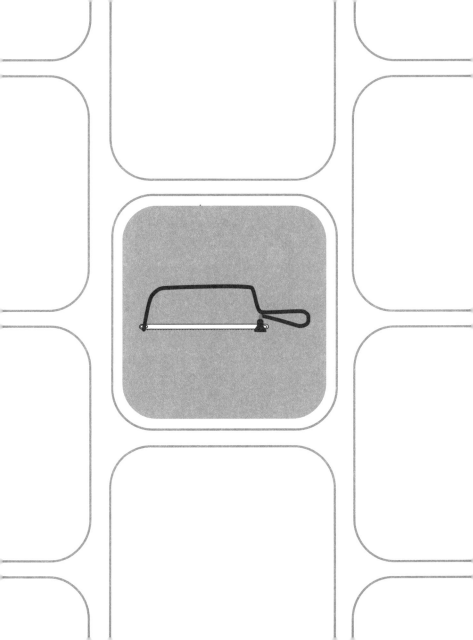

NAILING,
SCREWING
& GLUING

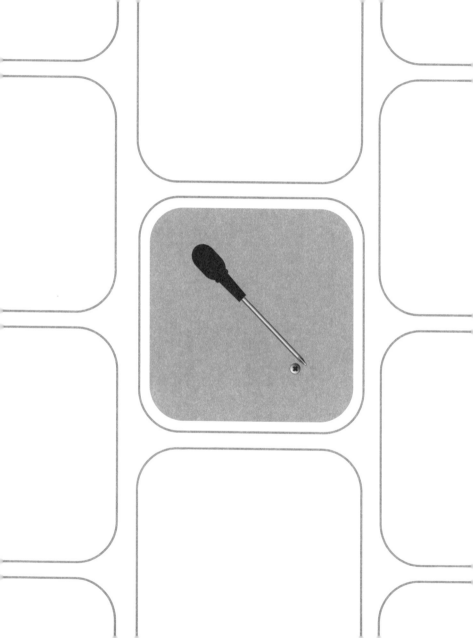

Join up here

Many do-it-yourself jobs involve attaching things to walls, securing things to other things, and joining things together. Most things are secured by means of screws, nails, bolts, glue, or, occasionally, double-sided adhesive tape. What you use for the job depends on:

FUNCTION: What's the thing I'm securing supposed to do?

MATERIAL: What's it made of?

SIZE: How big is the thing I'm securing?

LOAD-BEARING REQUIREMENTS: How much weight does it have to carry or how much stress will it be under?

AESTHETIC CONSIDERATIONS: How will it look?

Why choose nails?

✳ They're easy to use.

✳ They only require a hammer and a steady hand to knock them into place.

Which nail?

WIRE NAIL: Unless you're into serious building work you'll mostly use wire nails. The shaft has an oval cross-section and the nail has a solid, slim head.

LOST-HEAD NAILS: These have a head that isn't much wider than the shaft of the nail. They're less visible and can be knocked below the surface of the wood with a nail set.

TACKS: These are short, tapered, easy-to-use nails with a large head and a sharp point. They're mostly for securing carpet and fabric.

BRADS: These thin nails with a small head are used when screws would be too big and would split the wood, such as when you are installing panels or boxing in. They go in easily and are barely visible.

HANDYWOMAN NAILING TIP

Start nailing by holding the nail in position and giving it several short taps until it is in far enough to stay put. Then you can drive it in fully with heavier blows without endangering your thumb.

SHORTCUT TO NAILING SUCCESS

For very short nails or tacks where there is no room for fingers, push the nail into a small square of thin cardboard, which is easier to hold in position and can be torn away when the nail is firmly anchored in the wall.

Why choose screws?

✳ They provide a stronger grip and better support.

✳ They're easy to unscrew if you make a mistake, or want to take something down or move it to a different position.

✳ They're essential for installing panels that may need to be removed for access to plumbing, electrical cables, or gas pipes.

Did you know that...?

...screws are described by length, diameter, and threads per inch. The diameter is given in number sizes from #0 to #12, and for thicker screws in fractional inches. The size and length of screw you need depends on use—thicker and longer to bear a lot of weight, and slimmer ones for thinner, lighter materials.

Easy does it

Screwing into wood is relatively easy.
The thread of the screw digs its own made-
to-measure hole where it sits nice and tight.
Some screws have sharp points and special
threads for screwing directly into the wood,
but a pilot hole (see page 33) will make putting
them in much easier and more accurate.

Handywoman helpline

Q: I often can't seem to get the screw to tighten properly. What am I doing wrong?

A: If this happens, the screw may be too short or too thin for the hole, the hole may not be providing a suitable grip, the material you are screwing into may be too soft or too hard, or the anchor plug (see page 67) you're using may not be large enough.

Anchoring a screw when there's nothing to grip

To get screws to stay in, you must provide something for them to grip on to. This means you are going to have problems screwing into hollow walls, hollow doors, masonry, and drywall panels.

✳ Hollow-wall and door anchor bolts enable a screw to be fixed into a hollow wall or door where a normal screw and plug wouldn't work. You drill a hole, put the anchor bolt into it, and screw it tight. As you do so, the outer part of the bolt folds up against the inner face of the wall or panel to keep the screw firmly in place.

✳ For a screw to grip securely into masonry, you must use an anchor plug. These are commonly made of plastic and come in sizes to suit all screws. Make your hole with a drill and hammer the anchor plug into it (see page 37), then screw the screw in place. Make sure the screw goes into the center of the anchor plug and not over to one side.

✳ There are a number of other anchor plugs for use on soft masonry or on drywall panels. Threaded plugs will screw directly into the wall. Nailable plugs consist of a nail with a plug attached which is hammered into a predrilled hole.

Simple joints

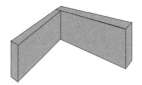

The simplest way to secure two pieces of wood together is with a butt joint, where two edges are butted together and secured with nails, screws, or wood glue. This kind of joint is fine if it's going to be covered up or painted.

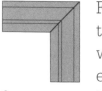

Plain baseboards can be joined using a simple butt joint.

For a job such as putting new trim around a door or securing wooden quadrant around a floor edge, a mitered joint is necessary for a neater finish.

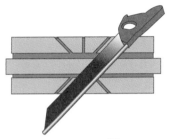

Making a mitered joint involves cutting an accurate 45-degree angle which can be constructed using simple math and a protractor or, if you are working on narrow strips of wood, a miter block. A miter block has 45-degree slots for accurate cuts.

Self-assembly setscrews

Setscrews are usually provided with self-assembly furniture. They're made specifically for the product so may look different from standard screws. For tightening them you need an Allen wrench. This fits snugly into a hexagonal socket in the head of a bolt and is then turned. These are usually supplied with the product but if not, you can buy an inexpensive set of several different sizes.

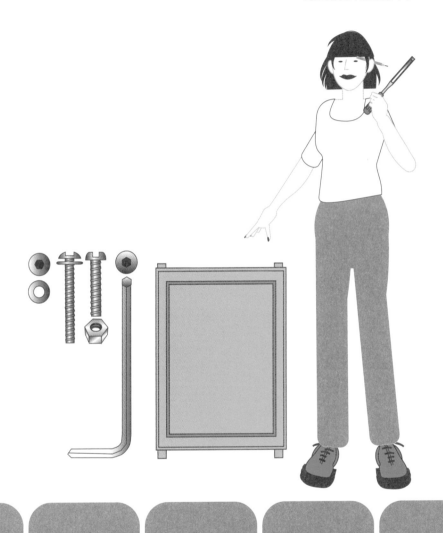

The pros of glue...

✳ Modern adhesives are very efficient.

✳ Some are strong enough to be used instead of nails or screws.

✳ They can be useful for poor-quality or hollow walls that may be unsuitable for screws or nails, or in places or situations such as an awkward corner or proximity to wiring or pipes, where putting in a nail or screw could be difficult or even dangerous.

✳ Wood adhesives can be used in addition to nails and screws to strengthen wood joints.

...and the cons

✸ Positioning must be accurate.

✸ It isn't easy handling and maneuvering long lengths of wood coated in quick-drying adhesive.

✸ Anything stuck down will be difficult to remove without damaging the item that is stuck and the surface it is stuck to, whereas nails and screws can be removed relatively easily.

Support boards

Securing a board to the wall—to which other items can be fixed—is a passport to greater things. Once you've done it you'll feel you've earned a certain amount of do-it-yourself cred. A secured board can be used to support shelving, worktops, cabinets, or other heavy weights such as a large picture. It can also be used as a framework for boxing in pipes or installing wall panels, and can be useful for attaching things to a hollow wall where the board can be screwed securely to solid wood studs. Or, if you like, it can simply be used to support a row of coat hooks.

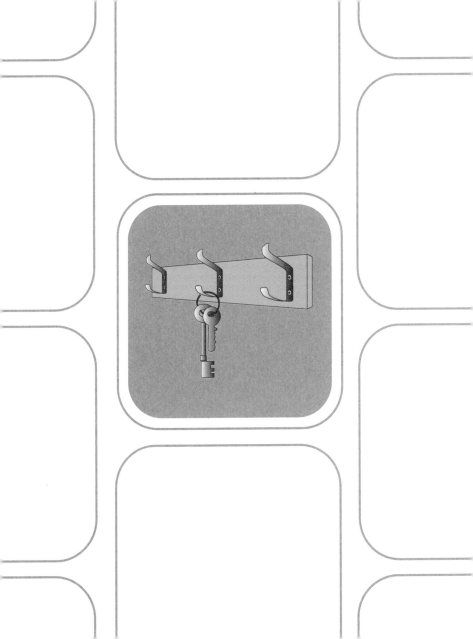

Securing a board

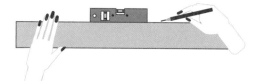

1 Cut the board to the length required. Hold it against the wall and use a carpenter's level to ensure that it's perfectly horizontal. Then draw a pencil line on the wall across the top and along the ends. Place the board on a work surface, mark the position of the screws, making sure they are evenly spaced, and drill through.

2 Place the batten support board against the wall and make an indentation mark in the wall through each hole.

3 Drill holes in the wall at the marks using a power drill. Insert an anchor plug in each drilled hole.

4 Secure the support board to the wall using screws that are long enough to go right through it and into the anchor plugs.

Six simple projects to do in a weekend

1 Sort out your music collection by putting up a wall-mounted CD rack.

2 Revamp the bathroom by installing new bathroom fixtures including a fresh toilet-paper holder.

3 Make a coat rack by screwing a row of simple clothes hooks to a board secured to the wall.

4 Keep your bathroom tidy by installing a new medicine cabinet, complete with mirror for those essential make-up checks.

5 Avoid last-minute searches for your house, car, or bicycle-lock keys by putting up a row of hooks on a board in the hallway next to the front door.

6 Decorate your walls by at last hanging up those heavy picture frames or mirrors.

PAINTING

Did you know that...?

...paint can completely change the look and mood of a room. It can make it look cleaner, bigger, cozier, sexier, or more stylish. It's also a well-known fact that when selling a house, a coat of paint can turn your home from impossible to incredible.

Handywoman helpline

Q: There's such a huge range of paints on the market that I never know where to start … and that's before I even think about choosing a color! Can you help?

A A water-based latex paint is best for internal walls. It's easy to apply and to wash out of brushes, rollers, and your hair. Available in flat or satin finish, latex paint also comes in a huge range of colors. What's more, it's quick-drying and hardly smells.

The dense chalky finish of distemper is historically correct and is particularly suitable for painting the internal walls of old properties. But it's less stable than latex paint and will rub off, so is unsuitable for areas of high wear such as staircases.

When it comes to woodwork, high-gloss paint is hardwearing but shows up all imperfections and needs careful application. Traditionally, high-gloss paint is oil-based and so is smelly and slow to dry, but water-based versions are now available.

Eggshell, satin, and soft-sheen paints are alternatives for woodwork. Some are now water-based. They're much easier to use than oil-based paint and won't show up every imperfection.

Paint with a dead mat finish is usually oil-based. It can be used on woodwork and plaster and papered walls as well.

How much paint?

✳ The amount of paint required for a job will depend on the type and make of paint, the color, state, and porosity of the existing surface, and the method of application.

✳ Details of estimated coverage will be printed on the container—usually in square feet or yards. One gallon of latext paint should cover about 330 square feet.

✳ Extra coats will be necessary to cover a dark color or pattern. Pure, deep colors, such as bright yellows or reds, will need extra coats, too.

All about brushes

✴ For painting walls, invest in a good-quality, flat 6-inch wide brush.

✴ For window and door trim, you'll need a range of narrower brushes, and for larger areas of woodwork, such as doors, you should have a slightly wider brush.

✴ Narrow cutting-in brushes have the bristles cut at an angle to make it easier to get right to the edge when painting window muntins.

✴ The very cheapest brushes—often sold in bargain sets—will shed their bristles and won't hold the paint well, so are best avoided.

✴ The most expensive brushes have high-quality, densely packed real bristles for ease of application and a smooth finish.

✳ Unless you're planning a lot of decorating (and are prepared to take great care of your brushes) go for a medium-priced range.

HANDYWOMAN BRUSH BUYING TIP
Check that the bristles spring back when you bend them.

HANDYWOMAN NEW BRUSH TIP
Some brushes shed a few bristles when they're new, so before using them on woodwork (where shedding bristles will spoil the finish) break them in by using with latex paint first.

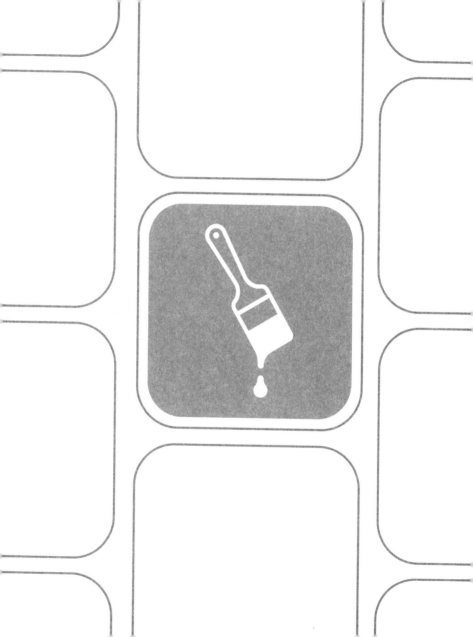

What a mess!

Painting is a messy business so make sure you have enough drop cloths to protect furniture, floors, and other surfaces from paint splashes and from the water and debris that is inevitable when you wash and strip down walls. Old sheets and bedspreads make adequate drop cloths but use plastic sheets underneath on vulnerable surfaces because big blobs of paint can soak through fabric.

Handywoman helpline

Q: Why do I always end up with the paint running down my hand when I'm painting and why do I usually get such a poor finish?

A: First of all, it's important not to overload the brush. Dip only a third of the bristles into the paint and wipe off any excess on the side of the container before painting. And when you paint, use vertical strokes—not dabs or sploshes—and spread the paint out using horizontal strokes as well. On large areas don't brush the paint out too thinly at the edges because this will contribute to your uneven finish.

Roll me over

✳ Rollers are fantastic for covering large areas of wall or ceiling quickly and evenly.

✳ Most paint-roller sleeves are either sheepskin (real or synthetic) or foam.

✳ Long-pile sheepskin holds a lot of paint but medium-pile is more manageable.

✳ Foam sleeves are less efficient because they tend to leave air bubbles on the surface.

✳ Paint roller and roller pan sets are often very inexpensive, and although the quality may not be tip-top, you can just throw them away after use.

✳ Long-handled roller extensions are helpful for painting ceilings and floors.

✳ Use a small roller on a long handle when you have to paint behind a radiator, a special shaped roller for painting into corners, and a small dense foam roller with gloss or eggshell paint for any large flat areas such as doors and bathtub panels.

Shortcut to roller success

Before painting walls and ceilings with a roller, do a little cutting in—using a small brush to paint around all the ceiling/wall joints, corners, baseboards, switches, and light fixtures. Then you can roll away to your heart's content.

Paint-pad perfection

Paint pads are very useful for painting large flat areas and are generally thought to be as good as a roller. They consist of a layer of short mohair pile attached to a foam layer, which gives flexibility and keeps the pad in contact with uneven surfaces. The pad is fixed to a plastic frame with an integrated handle. Also sold in sets with a tray, the best type of tray has a loading roller to ensure that the paint is distributed evenly on the pad.

To use, keep the pad flat against the surface and paint in all directions with a gentle sweeping action.

Eight must-have painting prep tools

Using the right tools makes preparation easier as well as more effective.

1 Scrapers or wallboard knives are used for removing wallpaper or paint. They have flat, nonflexible blades.

2 Contoured scrapers are useful for removing paint from awkward corners and moldings.

3 Wallpaper scorers are used to puncture the surface of coated or painted wallpaper.

4 Steam strippers are held against the wall so the steam penetrates the paper and makes it easier to remove.

Heat guns heat and soften solvent-based paint so it can be scraped off easily.

 Liquid wallpaper strippers break down the adhesive bond between the wallpaper and the wall.

 Scrubbing brushes are useful for cleaning dirt from corners.

 Dry paintbrushes can be used as dusting brushes to clean corners and keyholes.

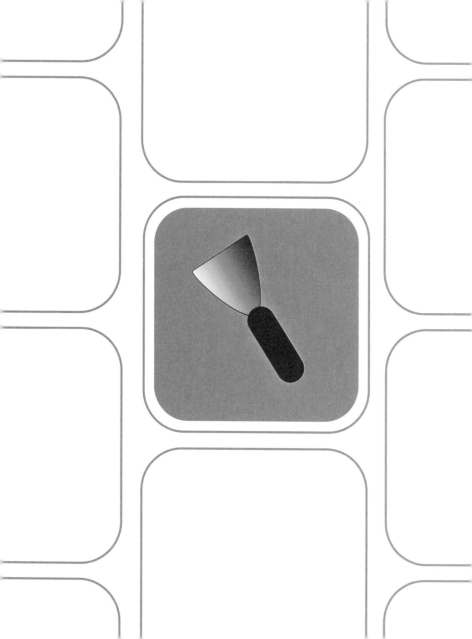

Get that paper off!

If you need to remove old wallpaper, find a hidden corner and remove a little to get an idea of how many layers there are, what type of paper it is, whether it'll come away easily, and the state of the wall beneath. If lots of plaster comes away with the paper, it may be best to leave it alone and paint over the top or get a professional to replaster.

Uncoated paper should come off easily with wallpaper stripper mixed with warm water, or by steaming. Coated wallpapers and paper that has been painted over will need scoring first with a wallpaper scorer or with the edge of a scraper. If the paper is vinyl-coated you can usually remove it by simply lifting the corners of the vinyl and pulling it away from its backing paper. The backing can then be removed with wallpaper stripper.

Wall prep

If the old paint surface has loose flakes of paint, use wet-and-dry paper to smooth their edges. Alternatively, use a nylon pan scourer. If, after filling in any holes and cracks (see page 182), the surface still looks flaky, you can give the wall a coat of general-purpose builder's sealer.

For sealing new or newly revealed bare plaster, you can use sealer or a diluted coat of latex paint.

HANDYWOMAN TIPS FOR UNEVEN WALLS
If, despite priming, sanding, and filling, your wall surface is still uneven, you can either learn to love the distressed effect or paint it with a roller to give a slightly textured finish that will soften the blemishes. Alternatively, cover the wall with a plain, thick, textured wallpaper and paint over it.

Six steps to perfect woodwork prep

 Wash down old woodwork using warm water and detergent.

 Get rid of blemishes and provide a key with a nylon pan scourer.

 Sand down any old drips and wrinkles.

 Hard gloss paint may need extra sanding with fine wet-and-dry paper.

Repair chips and damaged areas with primer, building up the surface with several coats if necessary and sanding lightly between each.

 Wipe down with a clean cloth dipped in mineral spirits to get rid of any remaining dust and grease.

HANDYWOMAN WALL AND CEILING STAIN TIP

Cover stains such as damp or mildew with a stain block or recommended primer, but address the source of the stain first to prevent the stains from reappearing.

If you cover a damp area with an impervious coating, it will only send the moisture elsewhere where it could do more damage.

Bare all

✳ When you use a heat gun to strip paint, make sure to keep it moving or you'll end up with burnt wood.

✳ Use a narrow nozzle on window muntins, to keep the heat away from the glass.

✳ When you use chemical paint stripper, follow the instructions, make sure there's good ventilation, and wear a protective mask and good protective gloves because the stripper burns the skin. Don't use it on large areas because the fumes are too overpowering.

✳ If you're stripping paint ready for repainting, a bit of residue is okay if it's sanded down and free of grease. But if you want the bare-wood look, you'll have to work hard to get every bit off. Use chemical paint stripper or a heat gun.

Primers and sealers

Special primers and sealers are used to prepare certain surfaces for painting.

STABILIZING PRIMER: A white or clear liquid used on walls to bind dusty, powdery, and flaky surfaces.

WOOD PRIMER: Available in solvent-based, water-based, acrylic, or aluminum forms. Used on new or bare wood to seal and prevent paint from soaking into the wood.

GENERAL-PURPOSE PRIMER: Used for wood, metal, and plaster as well as for porous building materials. Look for water-based versions.

METAL PRIMER: Prevents corrosion and provides a key for paint. Rust inhibitors are also available.

Undercover story

Undercoat paint is a mat coating that you can use on woodwork to cover primer as well as any minor imperfections. It provides a smooth, dense surface for your topcoat and is particularly effective if the topcoat is a dark color or has a high-gloss finish.

Ten handywoman painting tips

1 Work from right to left if you're right-handed (the other way around if you're left-handed) so that your arm is away from your body.

2 For woodwork, your brushstrokes should be vertical or horizontal (according to the direction of the grain of the wood) to prevent brushmarks from spoiling the finished surface.

3 For a neat line along baseboards, around door and window trim, and between ceiling and wall, place the brush a short distance away from the edge and press down so the bristles fan out to reach the edge.

Be careful not to disturb soft paint and don't try to neaten up edges until the paint is hard.

 For a high-quality finish on your woodwork, apply two or three topcoats and rub down carefully with steel wool or wet-and-dry paper between each coat.

 To avoid drips, runs, and sags, make sure there isn't too much paint on your brush/roller and brush or roll it out across the surface.

 Brush out any runs as you proceed, but don't attempt to do this once the surface has started to dry.

To avoid specks and lumps on the surface, make sure your brush is clean and that the surface is completely free of dirt and dust.

 During a break, put the lids on containers and put brushes, rollers, or pads (with their trays) inside a sealed plastic bag to prevent them from drying out and attracting dust.

 To avoid a patchy finish on walls, only take a break when an entire wall is complete.

"To avoid drips, make sure there isn't too much paint on your brush."

Clean up your act

✳ Try to clean brushes and other equipment as soon as you've finished work or the paint will harden and be more difficult to remove. If this isn't possible, then put them in a plastic bag or leave them to soak in water.

✳ For water-based paints, wash brushes, rollers, and pads in warm soapy water and rinse until the water is clear.

✳ For solvent-based paints, wipe off excess paint on newspaper then flex the bristles in a jar of mineral spirits or paint thinner to remove the rest. Wash with hot soapy water and rinse. Repeat until the brush is clean.

HANDYWOMAN KEEP-IN-SHAPE TIP
Keep paintbrushes in shape by folding paper around the bristles and securing with a rubber band.

PAPERING

Novice notes

✳ If you're a complete wallpapering novice, think very carefully before embarking on wallpapering a room. If the room is large, has high ceilings, is very irregular in shape, or has more than one window and door, it's better to hire a professional or stick to paint.

✳ For your first attempt, why not paper just one wall or a chimney breast? That way you avoid corners, overlaps and having to cut around light switches.

✳ Alternatively, start with a very small room with no awkward features and stick to wallpaper patterns that won't look obvious if they don't quite line up. Avoid wallpapering ceilings if possible.

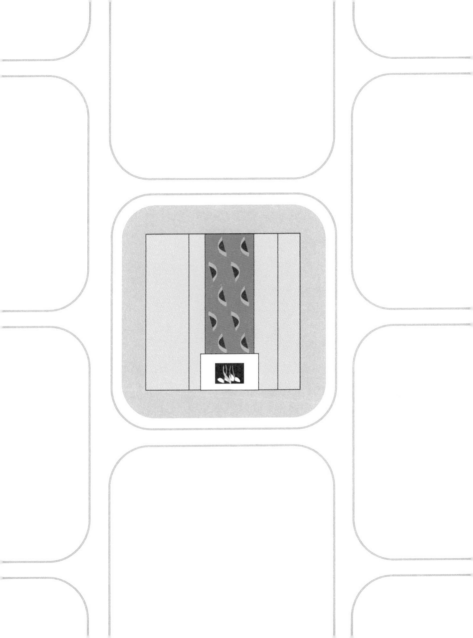

Wallpaper choices

LINING PAPER: Plain, buff-colored paper used over slightly uneven or impervious surfaces to create a suitable paint surface. Also used underneath heavy or expensive wallcoverings.

WOODCHIP PAPER: Made by sandwiching particles of wood between two layers of paper. Inexpensive and easy to hang, it covers poor plaster and uneven surfaces. Must be painted.

TEXTURED PAPER: Heavily embossed with a variety of patterns, from traditional designs to more modern, abstract ones. Rarely used on every wall; more often used below a dado rail or on a ceiling. Always painted.

PRINTED PAPER: An enormous range of designs and colors from small spriggy flowers to bold geometrics and famous designs from the past. The thickness and quality varies and will be reflected in the price.

PREPASTED PAPER: Some wallcoverings are precoated with an adhesive that is activated by soaking in cold water.

VINYL WALLCOVERING: Vinyl wallcovering has an impervious, washable surface suitable for bathrooms and kitchens. It consists of a paper or cotton backing with the pattern printed onto a vinyl coating and fused into the surface using heat. Often sold with preapplied adhesive.

WALLPAPER BORDERS: Borders of varying designs and widths are often intended for use with a coordinating paper but can be used on their own on a painted wall. Some are prepasted.

VINTAGE PAPERS: Specialty stores and street markets often sell rolls of original old wallpaper, especially from the fifties and sixties. It's rare to find a large quantity, but a small amount can become a fabulous focus of an interior.

Six wallpapering must-haves

1 **PASTING TABLE:** Cheap and very useful. It's the right size—just a little wider than the average roll of paper—and a good working height—slightly higher than a dining table. It's light and can be moved around easily.

2 **PASTING BRUSH:** Apply paste with a large paste brush or wall brush with soft, long bristles. Alternatively, use a short-pile paint roller and put the paste in the paint pan.

3 **PAPERHANGER'S SCISSORS:** These have extra-long blades for straight cuts, but any large pair of sharp scissors will work.

PAPERHANGER'S BRUSH: Like a wide paintbrush with a stumpy handle, this is for smoothing the paper onto the wall. The bristles must be soft enough not to damage the paper, but stiff enough to be poked into corners and force out excess paste.

SEAM ROLLER: A small wood or plastic roller that can be run up and down the seams to press down the paper so that it won't lift when dry. Rubber smoothing rollers squeeze trapped air from under the paper. Use a felt roller for delicate papers. Don't use a seam roller on textured paper.

RETRACTABLE TAPE MEASURE, PLUMB LINE, AND CARPENTER'S LEVEL: Essential for helping you to mark the position of the paper.

Handywoman helpline

Q: How on earth do I work out how much wallpaper I'll need for the job?

A: Wallpaper rolls come in various widths and lengths, but the most common size is 20½ inches wide by about 11 yards long. To calculate what you need, measure the wall height from ceiling to floor and add 4 inches extra for trimming to obtain the approximate drop length. Work out how many drops you can get from one roll. Measure around the perimeter of the room (ignoring windows and doors) to find out how many roll widths you will need. Divide this by the number of drops you can cut from one roll to give the number of rolls required. Add to this an allowance for matching any pattern (the repeat length will be given on the label) and add a little more for mistakes and accidents.

Some wallpaper rolls are labeled with the square feet they cover rather than width and length and for these you need to calculate how many square feet you need to cover. Look for calculating charts in the store.

Wallpaper prep

Prepare walls as for painting but seal newly plastered walls with a proprietary size or diluted wallpaper paste so that the wallpaper will stick.

Order of work

Finish painting ceilings and woodwork before hanging wallpaper.

Papering around a door

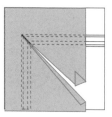

Allow a length of wallpaper to fall across the door then make a diagonal cut toward the corner of the door frame. Brush the paper into place along the side of the frame, then score with scissors around the frame and trim, leaving ½ inch along the top edge for the piece above the frame. Brush down the remaining paper above the door and trim along the top of the frame.

Papering around a window recess

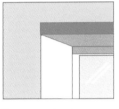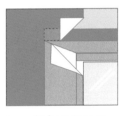

For a neat edge around a window recess, paper the top of the recess first, then paper over the overlap and cut along the edge as if you were papering around a door (see opposite).

Papering around a radiator

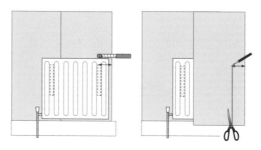

Mark the position of the radiator bracket and cut the paper from the bottom, up the length of the bracket. Push the paper into position around the bracket using a long-handled brush.

Papering around a switch or outlet

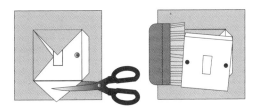

When you come to a switch or electrical outlet, allow the paper to fall across it (turn off the electricity first), push scissors through the paper at the center of the switch or outlet and make four diagonal cuts toward the corners. Tap the paper into place around the edge of the coverplate and trim off the excess, leaving ¼ inch all around. Unscrew the coverplate, tuck the paper behind, and screw back into position. Wait until the paste is dry before turning the electricity back on.

Did you know that...?

...thin paper will show up any small imperfections in the underlying surface and will highlight larger ones.

...uneven walls and less-than-straight edges will be emphasized by stripes or large patterns.

...damp walls are not good for wallpaper unless you can waterproof the surface beforehand with a special sealer.

...unless paper is vinyl coated, the surface will rub off in areas of high wear such as halls and staircases. Furniture will also damage the surface if allowed to rub against it.

...porous and noncolorfast papers are not suitable for kitchens or bathrooms or anywhere where they may come into contact with moisture.

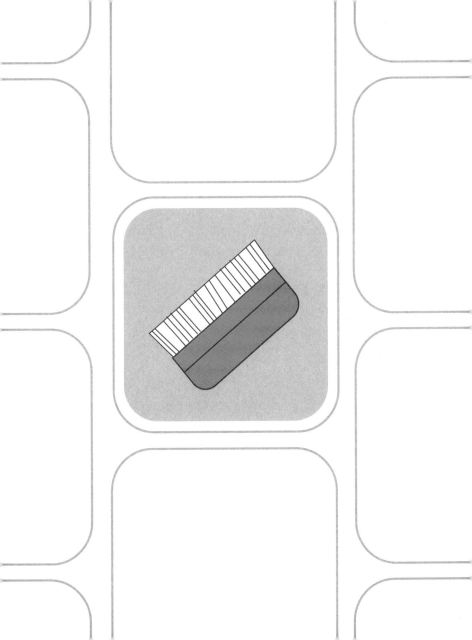

TILING

Seven tiling essentials

1 **SLIDING TILE CUTTER**: Used to score straight cuts along tiles for areas where full tiles won't fit. Directions for safe cutting come with the cutter.

2 **TILE NIPPERS**: Pincers used to cut narrow strips, small notches and corners from tiles.

3 **TILE SAW**: Used for cutting out curved shapes when fitting tiles around curved shapes such as pipes.

4 **METAL FILE AND TILE SANDER**: Used to smooth down cut edges.

TILE ADHESIVE: Usually sold premixed. Most are water-resistant.

PLASTIC SPACERS: Guides for spacing tiles accurately.

GROUT: Fills the gaps between tiles. Heat-resistant grouts for kitchens and epoxy-based grouts for germ-free worktops are available.

Handywoman helpline

Q: Yet again, I've got problems working out quantities. How can I calculate how many tiles I need for a job?

A: This isn't too difficult. Measure one of the tiles you'll be using and then work out how many you need for the height and the width of the area to be covered. Multiply the two figures and add 10 percent (15 percent for beginners) for breakages and mistakes.

Q: And what do I have to do to get the surface ready before I tile?

A: Tiles can be stuck to most surfaces as long as they're flat, clean, dry, and free of loose paint, plaster, or debris. Allow new plaster to dry completely before tiling. Don't tile over wallpaper. Prepare unstable surfaces with a coat of waterproof builder's sealer.

If you've got old tiles, you can remove them, which is messy and laborious, or you can tile on top. Scrape out any loose grout, stick down loose tiles, and fill big gaps with filler to prepare the surface.

Cutting a partial tile

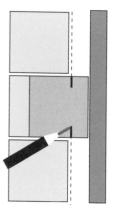

1 Set partial tiles at the edges after all the whole tiles are in position, and mark each one individually as the edges of the wall may not be straight. To mark the size of the tile, place it upside down on top of a tile in the last row of whole, fixed tiles and position it against the finished edge. Mark along the edge of the tile, not forgetting to make an allowance for the spacing and for any grouting if necessary.

2 Use the marks to cut the tile to size. Spread adhesive on the back and press into position.

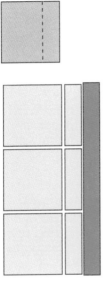

Tiling a backsplash

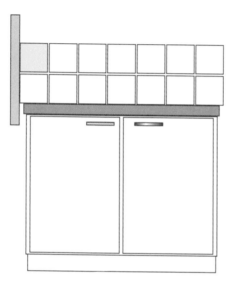

1 Measure and mark the position of the tiles and, using a board as a guide, work in rows starting in a top corner.

2 When tiling in a recess or lining the tiles up exactly with the edge of cabinets, mark the center line and work out toward the edges.

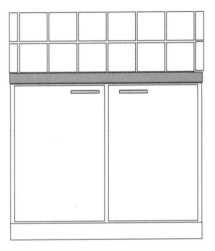

Tiling behind a cabinet

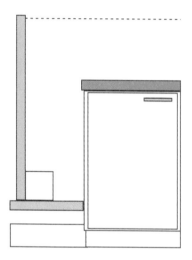

1 For tiled areas that extend beyond and around cabinets, place one board along the side and another along the line of the bottom of the lowest whole tile. Place the first tile where these boards meet.

2 Take away the board before measuring, cutting, and positioning the final edge tiles (see page 142).

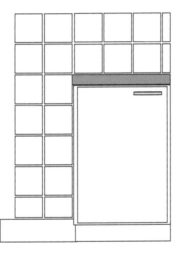

Grouting tiles

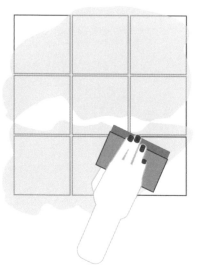

1 Allow 24 hours for the adhesive to harden before grouting. Using a rubber-bladed spreader or dense foam sponge, spread grout in all directions, forcing it into all the gaps. Wipe grout from the surface of the tiles using a barely damp sponge.

2 When the grout has dried, polish the tiles with a dry cloth.

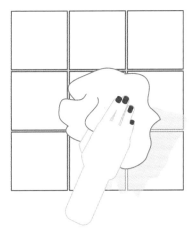

Setting mosaic tiles

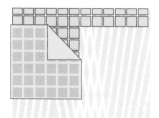

1 Mosaic tiles are usually supplied in sheets on a mesh backing or with a facing paper that is removed after application.

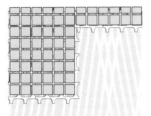

2 Keep the spaces between the sheets of mosaic the same as the space between individual tiles and fill in the edges by cutting strips or single tiles from the sheet using tile nippers.

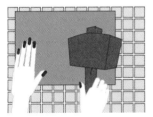

3 In order to make sure that the tiles are bedded properly, apply pressure with a piece of board covered in a soft material such as carpet, and tap gently with a wooden mallet.

Tiling around an outlet

When you tile around an electrical outlet or a switch you need to leave a space for the wiring. You also need to make absolutely sure that you're working safely and that means turning off the power before you start and not reconnecting it until everything has dried out. Follow these three simple steps for success.

1 Switch off the electricity, unscrew the coverplate, and pull it away from the wall. Position the tile or tiles on the wall where the outlet will be. Push the coverplate back as far as you can and mark the position of the outlet on the tiles in pencil.

2 Remove the tiles from the wall and cut them inside the pencil line so that when the outlet is back in place, there is room for the wires but the coverplate will sit on top of the tiles.

3 Set the tiles and grout. When the tile adhesive and grouting are completely dry, screw the outlet back in place and turn the power back on.

FLOORS, WALLS & CEILINGS

Bare is beautiful

... especially if it's limestone, old waxed boards, polished concrete, or brand new solid wood. Ordinary floorboards can look good when sanded, painted, varnished, or waxed. Old tiles, flagstones, and even concrete can look beautiful if cleaned and sealed.

but...

...bare floors can be cold, especially in winter—even with the best heating system.

...the ventilation under a wooden floor can create a draft if board gaps are too wide.

...bare floors are noisy, particularly when made of hard materials such as tiles that don't absorb any sound.

...before laying an impervious floor covering such as laminated planks or vinyl, make sure that it won't prevent air circulating below the floor as this can lead to rot.

Carpet pros and cons

✷ It's often less expensive and easier to carpet a room than to restore old floorboards.

✷ Wall-to-wall carpet is heavy and difficult to handle. Installing it and getting it neatly into corners isn't easy. A badly installed carpet will never look good, so maybe it's best to have the job done professionally.

✷ If finances are tight and you're desperate to cheer up a small room, then you can try installing carpet it yourself. Avoid expensive thick carpet and opt for thinner foam-backed carpet instead, then if it doesn't look perfect, you haven't wasted a fortune.

✷ Carpet is cozy to walk on.

✷ Carpet can cause allergies.

✷ Stains can be difficult to remove from carpet.

✷ Carpet helps with soundproofing.

Renovating floorboards

To renovate a wood floor, first clean it and check for damaged boards. If you want to replace a damaged floorboard, you have to match it to the others.

Inexpensive softwood floorboards, laid as a base rather than a feature, are usually thin and come in a standard width that's available from lumberyards and home-improvement stores.

Antique floorboards are often wider and thicker so you may have to go to an architectural salvage yard to find a replacement—and it may need a little cleaning up before use.

Replacing a floorboard

Lifting a floorboard should be done with care to avoid damaging the boards next to it.

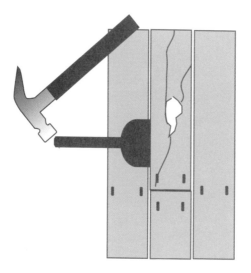

1 Tap the brick chisel into the gap near the end of the board to be removed. Lever gently until the board begins to lift and the nails start to come out.

2 Repeat this process at the other end. Insert the claw of a hammer under the lifted board to make room to insert a cold chisel.

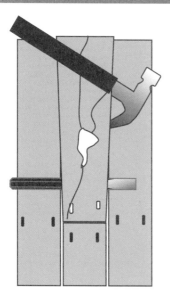

3 Slide the cold chisel underneath the floorboard toward the next set of nails. Repeat this process along the length of the board until it eases out.

4 Fit the new board into position and nail it down to the joist using floorboard nails. Nail at the ends and wherever it crosses a joist.

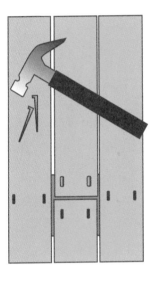

Five typical floor repair problems

If any of the following floorboard problems apply, you may want to seek help from a carpenter:

1 **PROBLEM:** The floorboard you want to replace disappears under the baseboard: you'll have to lift it up in order to pull it out. If it's a long board that extends under two baseboards, then you'll have to cut it in half.

2 **PROBLEM:** The floorboard you want to replace is nailed underneath the baseboard: you'll have to cut it as close to the baseboard as possible using a floorboard saw.

3 **PROBLEM:** The floorboards are tongued and grooved: there's no gap for easy levering.

PROBLEM: The new floorboard is thinner and sits below the rest of the floor: you will have to put packing underneath (cardboard, hardboard, or thin wood) where it is nailed to the joists.

PROBLEM: The new floorboard stands above the rest of the floor: you'll either have to make the board thinner by planing it or cut a recess into the joists to slot the board into.

Floor-sanding advice

✳ Sanding creates a lot of dust and noise, so warn your neighbors before you start work.

✳ Boards to be sanded must be sound, not too uneven and not full of holes.

✳ If you already have polished floorboards in good condition but feel they're a bit dull or dark, think hard before doing any sanding. Simply cleaning and re-waxing will lighten them and restore them to a glory you didn't know they had.

✳ Solid wood parquet floors should be left to the experts; don't risk spoiling them with home sanding.

✳ Before you start sanding, secure any loose floorboards and knock any protruding nail heads below the surface. Remove all furniture, drapes, and so forth and open all the

windows. Seal gaps around the door with tape and wedge in newspaper at the bottom. Hang a wet sheet on the outside of the door to help prevent the dust from escaping.

✳ Read the instructions that come with your rental floor-sanding machine and make sure you follow them carefully.

✳ Wear a mask, goggles, and ear protection.

✳ The sanding machine won't necessarily behave as you would expect it to. It will try to run away, so don't let go.

✳ Hold the drum off the floor when you switch it on and lower it gently to begin sanding. Once switched on, keep moving: leaving the sander in one spot for any length of time will result in a hollow in the floor.

Sanding a wooden floor

1 Using a coarse abrasive paper, sand the floor diagonally, tilting the machine to change direction and overlapping each run to ensure the whole surface is sanded. When you've done the whole floor, switch off, sweep up the dust, and start again, this time sanding diagonally in the opposite direction.

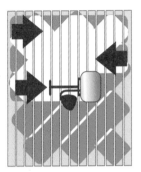

2 Once the floor is flat, change to a medium-grit paper and sand across the boards.

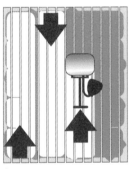

3 Using a fine-grit paper, sand up and down until the surface is smooth and scratch-free.

The perfect finish

Sealers for wooden floors divide roughly into varnishes and oils. Varnish can be applied by brush directly onto new or newly finished wood and will need two or more coats to form a hard, durable surface. Choose between a shiny or a mat finish. Sanding by hand between coats will give a better result.

Finishing oils soak into wood and plump up the fibers. Modern versions have additives to help form a waterproof and dirt-proof surface. Waxing on top of these will produce a soft, mellow finish that will mature well.

For less-than-perfect wood, a darker finish will disguise a multitude of sins. Avoid using wood stains as it can be difficult to achieve an even finish. Instead use a colored wood varnish. Most of these are available in different wood colors. Using a dark color will give a similar effect to a wood stain but with less hassle.

Stone

Stone or slate flags are full of character and add a sense of history, but they can also look stunning in a pared-down, modern interior. Damaged or pitted surfaces are part of their character. To restore, scrape off any old dirt or paint and scrub with soap and water or with a specialty stone cleaner. Fill any gaps using cement-based exterior crack filler, then finish with the appropriate sealer, which will soak into the stone and prevent dirt from penetrating.

Tile

Tiled floors are often found in old houses. If their condition isn't great, they may respond to a good clean, re-grout, and seal. You could freshen up a modern ceramic tiled floor by re-grouting with a new color.

Concrete

If you have an old concrete floor and like the brutal, industrial look, you can patch it up and paint it or simply seal it. Clean out holes and cracks, removing any loose material, then get rid of all the dust with a vacuum cleaner. Fill any gaps using cement-based exterior crack filler. Concrete is dusty, so you'll have to seal it if it's to be left uncovered.

Laying plank flooring

Prefinished laminated hardwood plank flooring comes in a range of veneers and prices. The planks fit together with tongue-and-groove joints for a seam-free surface.

New systems don't require adhesive. They can be laid on top of boards, concrete, or any level surface and usually come in kits that include spacers and a tamping block.

1 Cover the entire floor with foam backing, joining the strips together using adhesive tape. If the subfloor is made of concrete, lay down a thick sheet of plastic to prevent moisture rising up through the foam.

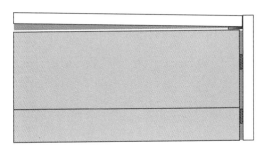

2 Place the grooved side of a plank along the longest wall. Put spacers in between to create an expansion gap. Insert the grooved side of a second strip into the first. Repeat until you are close to the wall. Cut the last strip to fit, allowing for an expansion gap.

3 Cut lengths of wooden quadrant to fit around the room to cover the expansion gap. Use a miter block to cut the angled joints for the corners (see page 69). Nail the quadrant in place with brads.

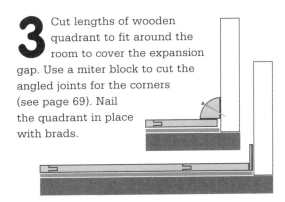

Handywoman helpline

Q: A wall's just a wall isn't it? Why do I need to know if it's anything special?

A: There are lots of different types and you need to know what you've got. First come solid walls—stone, brick, concrete block, or solid concrete. Inside walls are usually covered with plaster.

Old homes may have inside walls of lathe—strips of wood nailed to a framework and covered with lime-based plaster. Depending on the building's condition, this can be hard and strong or weak and crumbly.

A cavity wall is a double external wall with a gap in between which may be filled with insulation material.

A stud partition wall is a wooden framework with drywall panels nailed to it. This is often skimmed with a thin layer of plaster to give a smooth finish.

Then there are structural walls and nonstructural walls. Structural walls support a building. If you want to remove one, you need to replace it, usually with an I-beam (rolled steel joist). Definitely a job for the professional!

Nonstructural walls can be taken away without the building falling down. However, only an expert will know which walls are nonstructural, so DON'T try to do it yourself.

Warning signs

Very uneven, undulating surfaces on walls and ceilings are part of the character of an old property but in newer buildings it could be a sign of something wrong, so have them checked.

Fine cracks in plaster are often the result of shrinkage due to drying, heat, and so on, or vibration from impact such as knocking in nails or drilling a hole. Bigger cracks appear through settlement due to minor building work in adjacent rooms or properties, or are the result of unusually extreme temperatures. Large cracks or cracks that keep getting bigger can indicate structural faults, so get a professional to have a look.

Ceiling special

✳ If you're a novice, don't drill into a ceiling. There will certainly be electric wires and maybe heating and water pipes, plus ceilings aren't usually solid, which makes the whole procedure a risky business.

✳ Ceilings usually consist of drywall panels nailed to wooden joists. The drywall is then plastered. In old houses the plaster is applied to lathe (see page 179) and the plaster may be thick enough for a fairly deep hole. If you want to attach something to a new, thin drywall ceiling, use a threaded anchor plug.

✳ If you want to hang something heavy from the ceiling you have to find a joist to give you something solid to screw into. Tap along the ceiling until you find an area that doesn't sound hollow. If this extends right across the ceiling, then you've probably found a joist.

The whole truth

✳ Working on holes in ceilings gives you a pain in the neck.

✳ Small to medium-size cracks, holes, and dents in walls and ceilings can be filled using an all-purpose spackling compound. Apply it using a wide-blade putty knife or a wallboard knife and leave the compound slightly higher than the surrounding surface since it will shrink slightly when it dries. Once dry, use sandpaper to smooth out the bumps.

✳ For bigger, deeper holes use patching plaster and a latex bonding agent between coats. When it's dry, smooth with sandpaper.

✳ Seriously big holes usually involve some replastering. If you value your home and your sanity, call in an expert plasterer.

✳ Getting spackling compound into the gaps around door and window frames, baseboards, and the joints between walls and ceilings can be difficult, so use silicon caulk and a caulk gun.

Shortcut to hole-filling success

Old screw holes are often deep, so poke some pieces of damp newspaper into the hole before applying the spackling compound.

WINDOWS
& DOORS

Squeaky doors

Squeaky doors may provide atmosphere in a horror film but they're irritating. A squirt of oil on the hinges will solve the problem. If this doesn't work, or only works for a short time, it might be that the door isn't hanging correctly (see page 189).

Rattling doors

If the door rattles and doesn't close properly, it could be that the latch bolt doesn't fit into the strike plate. If this is the case, take off the strike plate and pack it out with some cardboard or wood filler, remembering that you may need slightly longer screws when you put it back.

Alternatively, the strike plate may be too close and the latch bolt doesn't have room to spring into the cavity, in which case remove the strike plate and chisel out a little more wood from the recess before screwing it back in place.

Handywoman helpline

Q: My door doesn't seem to fit the frame properly. Do I have to take the door off to make it fit better?

A: Not necessarily. Look at the hinges and check that the screws are all present and tight, that the hinges fit flush with the frame and that they're positioned so that the door hangs at 90 degrees. Sometimes the screws work loose and tightening them, or replacing them with slightly longer screws, will pull the door back into position.

If the door still won't shut, find the place where it isn't fitting into the frame and either sand it down or plane off the excess (you may have to take the door off to do this). ALWAYS make adjustments to the door, NOT the frame.

Door hinges

 ✳ The simplest form of hinge is the butt hinge with two flat rectangular flaps on each side of the knuckle. One is screwed to the inside of the door frame and the other to the edge of the door. They're set into a recess cut to the size and depth of the hinge flap so that they're flush with the woodwork. Just undo the screws on the frame if you need to remove the door.

 ✳ The rising butt hinge lifts the door as it opens to fit over any carpet. The hinge has two sections: one has a spindle and goes on the frame, the other a socket that fits over the spindle. The door can be lifted off without undoing any screws. They come in left- and right-handed opening versions.

Shortcut to hinge success

Worn hinges cause doors to drop and therefore stick. Fitting new hinges of the same size into the existing recess is easy, but use new, slightly larger screws to ensure that they fit tightly into the old holes.

Hanging a new door

1 First, find a friend to help hold the door in position. Make sure the door fits into the frame—there should be a gap of ⅟₁₆ inch at the top and sides and a minimum of ¼ inch at the bottom (more if you have thick carpet). To check, stand the door in the frame with wedges underneath to raise the door to the correct height.

2 Make any necessary adjustments to the door edges using a plane. With the door in the correct place, mark the position of the butt hinges 7 inches from the top and 10 inches from the bottom on both the door and the frame.

3 Stand the door on its edge with the hinge side uppermost. Place the flap of the opened hinge against the marks, making sure that the knuckle of the hinge projects beyond the edge. Draw around the flap with a pencil and mark the depth along the edge.

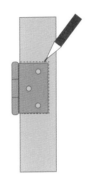

4 Use a chisel to make several cuts (the depth of the hinge) across the marked area, being careful not to cut across the pencil line. Also make cuts around the edge.

5 Pare away the wood to form a recess to fit the hinge flap.

6 Neaten the finished cut section. Repeat for the other hinge.

7 Put the hinge flap in place and mark and drill pilot holes for the screws.

8 Screw the hinge in place.

9 Wedge the door in an open position with the unscrewed flaps against the marks on the door frame. Making sure the knuckle is parallel to the frame, mark around the flap and repeat the carpentry on the frame.

10 Hang the door first using only one screw in each hinge and make sure the door opens and closes smoothly. You may need to make the recesses a little deeper, or pack them out with cardboard. Screw in the other screws.

Different types of windows

✳ Old double-hung windows go up and down by means of a cord in the side of the frame. New versions have a spring-mounted mechanism.

✳ Casement windows are hinged vertically to open like a door.

✳ Pivot windows have a hinge that allows them to rotate.

The guillotine effect

Broken sash cords won't prevent you from opening a double-hung window but they won't hold the window open either. Replacing them involves taking the window out of the frame so get someone who has done it before to help you. Watch how it's done, then you'll be able to replace the next one yourself.

What's it made of?

Most domestic window frames are made from wood but metal isn't uncommon. Many new frames are made from coated aluminum while others combine wood and metal in units whose construction is surprisingly complicated, so don't even think about taking one out or putting in a new one. They're designed to be virtually maintenance-free so shouldn't require much repair work; if they do, it's best to call in a window expert.

Play it safe

Broken or cracked windows are dangerous and insecure as well as looking unkempt and unloved. Get a professional glazier to replace any glass. A professional will measure correctly for the replacement, get it cut, take out the broken pieces, install the new glass, and take all the broken glass away. It's worth the money.

If you have those new metal window frames with the glass set into the frame, the glass requires special installation.

An open and shut case

✳ Windows that open and close easily are a joy. If they don't, it's often over-enthusiastic use of paint either inside or out that prevents them. If the paint is thin, you can carefully cut along the joint with a sharp-bladed knife and use a scraper to open up the gap. If it's thick and has seeped through all the joints, you'll have to resort to paint stripper or a heat gun (see page 107).

✳ If you can't shut the window properly, check where it fits against the frame—especially the hinge edge since paint or dirt may be preventing a good seal. Hinges may also stiffen as a result of overpainting. A small amount of paint stripper may help get things moving. A squirt of oil will also loosen up clogged hinges.

Five handywoman weatherproofing tips

1 The least expensive way to eliminate drafts is to install flexible foam weather stripping. It has a peel-off backing and is stuck to the door or window frame. It works well but gets grubby quickly and will need to be replaced regularly.

2 Many draft eliminators for doors take the form of wood, metal, rubber, plastic, or bristles attached to a strip (usually alumiium) that's screwed to the door frame.

3 Threshold weather strips are screwed along the bottom of the door either on the inside or out-side. These include weather trims (screwed to the outside of the door and angled to shed water) and brush seals (a row of dense stiff bristles attached to a metal or wooden trim screwed to the inside of the door).

4 To prevent drafts getting in through gaps between baseboards and floorboards, and around outdoor spigots, cables, and telephone lines, spray in expandable foam.

5 Weatherproofing for windows is much the same as for doors and varies according to the window type and construction. If any solution seems too expensive or will spoil the look of a window or door, consider keeping out drafts with heavy curtains or shades.

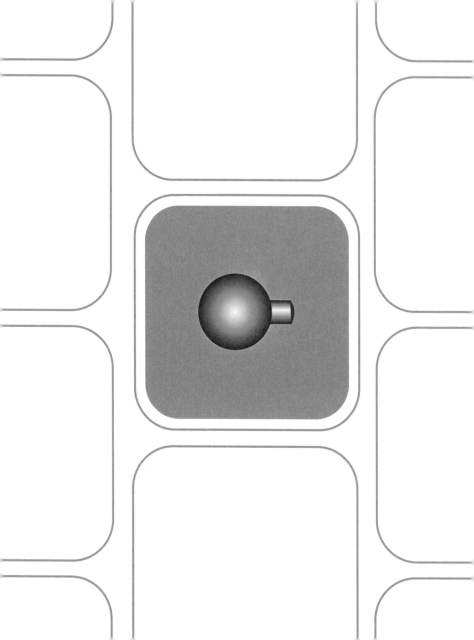

Shortcuts to door hardware success

You can transform an otherwise plain door by installing smart new door hardware. Choose from the wide range of traditional or modern designs.

Before buying, make sure you have the correct hardware for your door. The mechanism should either be fitted in a hole in the edge of the door or contained in a casing fitted on the surface of the door, with a strike plate screwed to the edge of the door frame.

Safe as houses

✳ Some home insurance companies insist on a certain level of security before providing cover. Find out before embarking on any security improvements since certain locks may be specified.

✳ Once you're inside with all the bolts and locks secured you won't be able to get out easily. Having to fiddle with keys in a fire could be fatal, and if you're ill, valuable time could be wasted by people who are trying to get to you.

✳ Make sure keys are kept in an accessible place (but not handy for burglars), leave a spare set with someone reliable, and give all details to close friends and family.

Did you know that...?

...window locks are often required for insurance purposes. They work by locking the window to the frame (or in the case of double-hung windows, by locking the windows together) either with a screw or a bolt. They are usually operated with a key. Many use a standard key, which is widely available, but others have keys that come in several hundred variations.

...newer windows are supplied with integral locks and lockable stays. If you have traditional, wooden windows, it's easy to install screw-on locks.

...patio doors are especially inviting to intruders, so make sure they're fitted with the correct type of lock and install them top and bottom to prevent the doors being lifted out of the frame.

Lock, stock, and barrel

✷ **LOCKS** are best installed by a locksmith but if you're simply replacing a lock, it's easy to do providing you get one of similar size and made to fit into the existing holes.

✷ **THE INTERNAL MECHANISM** is all you have to replace—not the entire lock—if your keys have been lost or stolen.

✷ **A CYLINDER RIM LOCK** is used mainly on front doors. A small knob or handle on the inside turns a spring lock to open the door. When the door closes, the spring lock automatically springs back into place and can only be opened from the outside using a key. An extra turn with the key from the outside will deadbolt lock it into position so that it can't be opened from the inside.

✷ **A MORTISE LOCK** is fitted into a hole in the edge of the door frame and must be locked and unlocked with a key, although some can be opened from the inside with a knob or handle.

✳ **HINGE BOLTS** screw into the edge of the door—near the hinges for strength—and fit into a recess in the door frame when the door is closed.

✳ **RACK BOLTS** fit into the edge of the door and are operated by a key.

✳ **SPYHOLES** are useful for checking out a visitor before choosing whether or not to open the door. They're simple to install and can be adjusted to fit any thickness of door.

✳ **A SECURITY CHAIN** is another wise precaution. The fixed end of the chain is screwed to the door frame and the loose end fits into a fixing plate screwed to the door. For convenience, position it just below the lock.

A welter of window treatments

✳ If you like the pared-down look (and aren't overlooked), leave your windows unadorned. If you value your privacy, use etched glass, plastic film, or a spray-on frosted-glass-effect paint.

✳ When it comes to drapes, gathers are out. The newest draperies are simple panels, just a tad wider than the window, and they hang straight from ungathered tops.

✳ Cropped curtains or drapes are all the rage. No need to have them touching the windowsill or hovering just above the carpet; let them hang out halfway between the window ledge and the floor.

✳ Hang drapes, panels, dhurries, or throws from simple poles and attach them with rings, ties, loops, clips, or even safety pins.

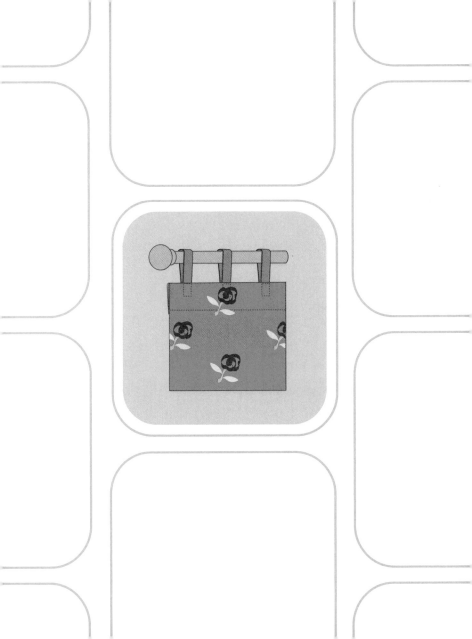

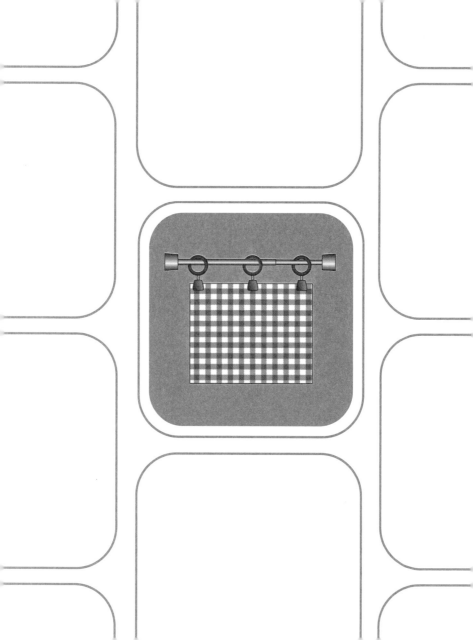

✳ Original old shutters enhance the character of a home. If you don't have them, try perfectly plain ultra-modern shutters or slatted versions instead, which look pleasingly European or a little colonial.

✳ Make lightweight shutters by stretching fabric onto a frame or threading panels onto poles. Use screw hooks and eyes to secure them in place.

FURNITURE
& SHELVING

Handywoman helpline

Q: I've got a lot of things that need to be stored on shelves but there's so much choice in the stores that my mind goes blank just thinking about it. How can I decide what's best for my purposes?

A: The shelving system you choose will depend on the state of the wall where you want your shelves and what you want to store. Stud partition walls (see page 179) can't support heavy shelves or heavy loads unless you can screw the supports or brackets into the wooden framework. The walls of old houses may be too soft and crumbly to hold screws securely and drilling into stone isn't easy. Some homes have concrete walls that require a very powerful drill for even the smallest job. If drilling into the wall isn't an option, it may be best to choose a freestanding system.

The lowdown on shelving materials

✱ Softwoods such as pine are relatively inexpensive and can be stained and sealed or painted.

✱ Hardwoods such as oak and beech look wonderful but are more expensive and heavier than other shelving materials.

✱ Board made of strips or blocks of solid wood glued together to form a knot-free surface is suitable for sealing or painting.

✱ Plywood is thin layers of wood sandwiched together and glued into sheets. Good for shelves, but should be cut by machine—and the edges will need careful finishing.

✱ Laminated boards are made of chipboard covered with laminate or veneer. Light, convenient, and inexpensive.

✳ Stainless steel and wire mesh are great shelving materials but buy them precut and finished as they're difficult to work with.

✳ If you're using glass, always buy the toughened type and get it cut and finished by a glass supplier.

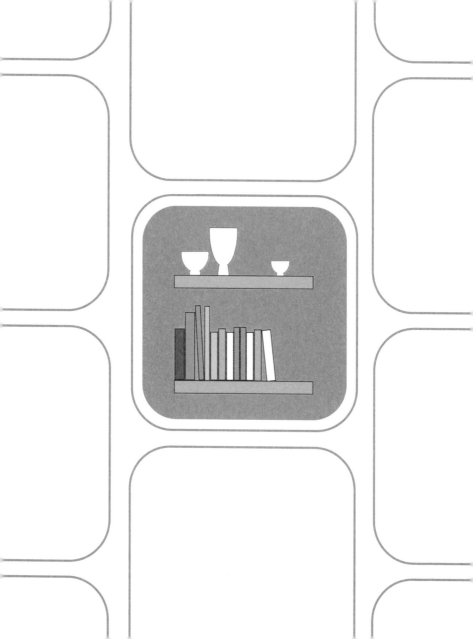

No visible means of support

The floating shelf, one of the most popular of the ready-to-hang types of shelf, is a boxlike construction with a hanging system that's entirely concealed within the construction so that the shelf looks as if it's floating. It looks very smart and can be surprisingly inexpensive. Installing one involves screwing a support board to the wall and securing the shelf to the board from underneath.

Go it alone

There are a variety of freestanding shelving systems around from very inexpensive wooden or metal units for garage or utility room storage to smarter combinations using high-quality materials. They're ideal if your walls aren't suitable for drilling into, or if you don't want or aren't allowed to drill into them. They are also easy to take down and re-assemble in a different position according to need or whim, and they can be used as room dividers.

A brace of brackets

✳ Pressed-steel shelf brackets are inexpensive and can look very chic in a contemporary "industrial" sort of way.

✳ Look out for smarter designs in stainless steel and curved plywood.

✳ Use large, chunky brackets and a thick plank of wood as a feature shelf.

✳ Use several brackets to support a long shelf. The shelf could even extend around the whole room.

Shortcut to shelving success

Shelving systems using brackets that slot into metal uprights screwed into the wall are flexible and involve less drilling.

Four handywoman tips for getting shelving right

1 When installing shelves inside alcoves, take measurements at the back, front, and all the way down the alcove as walls are rarely true.

2 Unless you want an exact fit, get all the shelves for an alcove cut to the smallest measurement.

3 To ensure adequate support when putting shelves on brackets, make sure that the bracket spans nearly the whole depth of the shelf and that there's sufficient overhang on each side. The amount of overhang will depend on the thickness of the shelf and the weight of the load.

Always use a carpenter's level for marking and positioning shelves so that they're level. A sloping ceiling and walls may make the shelf look "out," but lining it up with anything other than the true horizontal and vertical will lead to problems that are structural as well as visual.

Make your own picture shelf

Picture shelves allow you to change the arrangement of favorite artworks without peppering the wall with holes. Large pictures look stunning displayed this way but the shelf needs to be strong and well supported. Make the shelf slightly narrower than the back panel and make lipping that overlaps both edges of the shelf. This provides extra structural strength as well as a ledge against which the pictures can rest.

1 Cut three pieces of wood—a back panel, a shelf, and front lipping. For a shelf strong enough to hold pictures in frames, use a back panel that's no less than ¾ inch thick and 4–5 inches wide.

2 Drill pilot holes in the back panel ready for screws to fix it to the wall, then screw and glue it to the shelf for strength.

3 Place the lipping along the front of the shelf, then pin and glue into place.

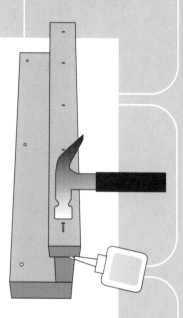

4 Fill over the pin heads, smooth the surfaces and edges with abrasive paper and paint or stain before fixing in place on the wall.

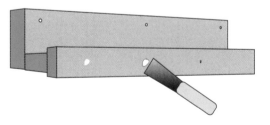

Five steps to installing a shelf on brackets

1 Mark the position of the shelf on the wall then work out the position of the brackets, allowing for the overhang. If you're using more than two brackets, space them evenly along the length of the shelf, measuring from the center for accuracy.

2 Hold one bracket on the wall using a level to ensure it's straight and mark the positions of the holes.

3 Drill the holes and screw the bracket to the wall.

4 Hold the next bracket against the wall on its marked position.

5 Place the shelf across both brackets, put a level on top, and adjust the position of the second bracket until the shelf is plumb. Mark the hole positions and secure as before. If you're using more than two brackets, secure the end ones first.

Off-the-shelf shelves

A variety of ready-to-hang shelves are now available. Some incorporate extras such as hanging rails, plate racks, and so forth, while others are plain but are made from materials such as wire mesh, stainless steel, or plastic— materials that a do-it-youselfer would have difficulty working with. Most can be secured directly to the wall with screws, so require nothing more than a drill and a carpenter's level to put them up.

"Off-the-shelf shelves require nothing more than a drill and a carpenter's level to put them up."

Be flexible

The simplest adjustable shelving systems consist of narrow metal standards with slots along their whole length into which purpose-made metal brackets are inserted.

1 To work out where the standards need to be positioned, secure the first standard to the wall with the top screw only. Using a carpenter's level to ensure that it's vertical, mark the positions of the other screws.

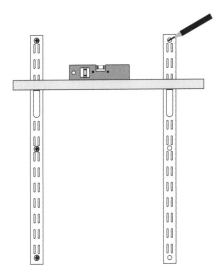

2 Drill at the marked points and screw the first standard to the wall. Insert a bracket near the top of the fixed standard and another in the corresponding position on a second standard. Hold this standard roughly where it's to be screwed to the wall. Place a shelf across the two brackets and move the standard into the correct position using a level. Mark the top hole, then drill and secure as before.

Shelves on support boards

Where shelves span two walls, they can be secured to support boards screwed to the walls.

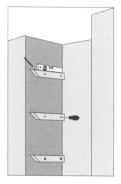

1 Cut the support boards to the required length, sand the edges, and cut the ends at an angle.

2 Drill pilot holes right through the support boards, using a countersink bit to hide the screws. Work out the position of each shelf and mark the position of the boards on one wall only, using a carpenter's level to check that they're plumb.

3 Starting at the top, secure the first support board to the wall, then place the shelf in position on it and on a second support board held in place on the opposite wall. When you are satisfied the shelf is level, mark the position of the second support board with a pencil line or with a bradawl poked through predrilled pilot holes.

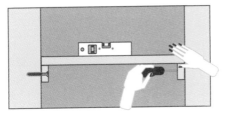

Metal support strips

Extruded aluminum support strips are an alternative to wood. The strip will usually be cut the full depth of the shelf and will therefore be visible at the front, giving a neat, modern feel. The installation and suitability for heavy loads will vary according to the design and make.

Make your own lipped shelving

For a neat look, fix an edging along the front of your shelves. Measure the alcove depth accurately, then cut the support boards and shelves short of the outside edge so that when the lipping is added it's flush with the wall.

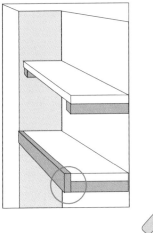

Attach the lipping with long brads, tapping
them well in so they can be concealed with
wood filler before they are sealed or painted.

Self-assembly furniture kits

TAKE YOUR TIME: This is the first rule. It always takes longer than you think.

MAKE IT FUN: Plan a day around it: have some good snacks at hand, but avoid alcohol—save that for the celebration or, in extreme circumstances, to forget any disasters afterward. Don't attempt it if you are feeling grumpy, and don't invite lots of people to help. You just need one other person because two sets of arms and hands can be useful.

ROOM FOR MANEUVER: Allow plenty of space and if the piece of furniture is very large, make sure you will be able to get it into the room it is destined for.

THE RIGHT TOOLS: Make sure you have what you need. Some tools will be included with the kit but you may need screwdrivers, wrenches, and clamps.

WHAT'S INSIDE?: Unpack carefully. (Examine all the pieces for damage and if any are damaged, pack it all up again and take it back.) If you are lucky, there will be a list of components and a sheet of instructions. Make sure the pieces look like those in the diagram and that you understand what each is and what it is for.

STILL COUNTING: Count the screws, bolts, and other fittings, and make sure they correspond with the directions. Sometimes extra screws are included—make sure you are aware of this to avoid the panic induced by the sight of two large screws glinting ominously alongside what's an apparently fully assembled piece of furniture.

BOXING CLEVER: Avoid tearing the cardboard box, keep it, open it out, and use it to work on. It will protect the parts—and the floor—from accidental scratches.

Make your own daybed on castors

A good-looking, strong daybed is simple to make using robust castors screwed to a solid-core fireproof door. This is strong enough to withstand a heavy weight and thick enough to hold the castors securely. Choose swivel-type castors that have reasonably large wheels and preferably rubber tires.

1 Use six castors for strength. Mark their positions accurately and don't put them too near the edges.

2 Screw the castors in place. Check they move freely and that the base is level. If the castor fitting is deeper than the base, screw blocks of wood to the base first.

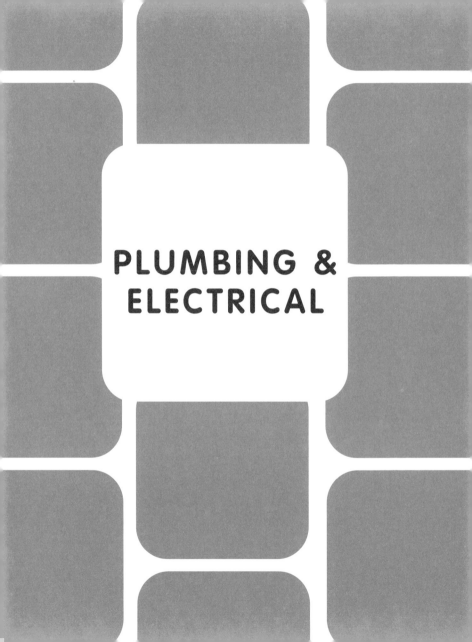

PLUMBING &
ELECTRICAL

Don't do it yourself

The installation and maintenance of hot-water systems and furnaces are subject to strict regulations. Any major work should always be carried out by a registered installer—failure to do this could affect any insurance claim should an accident occur. Never touch anything involving your gas or oil supply connection; the consequences of getting it wrong can be catastrophic. Always employ a registered professional.

Plumbing know-how

Most homes are connected to a main water supply that enters the house through the main shut-off valve (see page 255). Water is then distributed via a system of pipes to heating systems, tanks, faucets, and appliances such as washing machines and dishwashers.

Always speak to your local Building Department about Codes before beginning any major plumbing work. Codes vary from state to state and city to city, so if you have moved recently don't assume you know the plumbing rules.

Handywoman helpline

Q: Why have I got good water pressure down in my kitchen, but the water comes out with less pressure in the upstairs basins and shower?

A: Water pressure is usually strong in parts of the system that are near the main supply but can be less powerful on upper stories, especially if the boiler is several stories below. If lack of pressure is a problem, ask the advice of a good plumber who may suggest new plumbing, the re-siting of a water tank or the installation of a pump.

Where does it all go?

All waste is channeled to the sewer line. Bathtubs, showers, washing machines, sinks, toilets, and dishwashers eventually drain into a single main waste and vent stack that leads to the main sewer line (or if your are in the country, into your septic tank). The roof vent on the drain system allows air in to help the water flow out freely.

Is your house trying to tell you something?

Minor incidents such as a dripping tap or a blown fuse are irritating but not life-threatening and can be easily remedied. However, they can also be an indication of something wrong with the plumbing or electrical system or a worse problem elsewhere. If you often have to replace fuses or light bulbs, it could be due to a fault in the wiring. And if the sound of a dripping tap doesn't drive you mad, the realization that the drips have seeped through somewhere and formed an extremely large puddle will.

Need to know basis

You need to know where your main shut-off valve is located. This is your first port of call if you have a leak because it enables you to turn off the water supply right away. Usually the valve is found where the supply enters your home. You will also have shut-off valves for specific parts of the system, such as individual sinks, the washing machine, and so on.

Problems with your waterworks

✳ In case of a sudden and dramatic leak, turn off the shut-off valve right away. If the source of the leak isn't immediately apparent, call a plumber.

✳ Hairline cracks in pipes are difficult to detect and as the leaked water often travels along the outside of the pipe before dripping off, the location of the wet patch doesn't always coincide with the leak. If possible, repair the pipe temporarily by binding it with plumbing tape, then hire a plumber.

✳ Water can get through extremely small gaps such as the silicone caulk around bathtubs and sinks. Remove all traces of old caulk using a special solvent and replace, making sure that all surfaces are perfectly dry when applying.

✳ Areas behind bathtub panels, sinks, washing machines, and dishwashers are particularly vulnerable to leaks, so take a look from time to time. Common causes are loose fittings, worn threads, and worn washers. Try tightening joints using water-pump pliers if necessary (but don't force them).

HANDYWOMAN BATHTIME TIP

When sealing a joint around a bathtub, fill it with water and leave until the caulk has set. If you don't, the combined weight of water and bather will pull the sealant away from the wall and break the seal.

Drip, drip!

The most common reason for a faucet to drip is a worn washer. If you have a traditional faucet, then changing a washer isn't complicated.

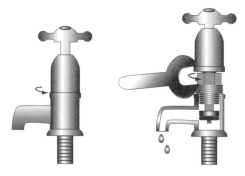

1 Turn off the water at the shut-off valve. Unscrew the cover and lift to reveal the retaining nut, then unscrew this using water-pump pliers. (Not all old faucets look the same, but the basic system will be similar.)

2

Lift out the top section of the faucet, remove the old washer, and replace with a new one of the correct size.

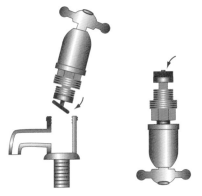

Four ways to clear a blockage

1 Sinks usually have a plastic drain trap with slip nuts that can be unscrewed to allow blockages to be cleared.

2 There may also be a slip nut on the branch pipe, which can be cleared using a wire coat hanger.

3 A caustic drain cleaner will shift blockages but should be used with care. Follow the instructions on the packet.

4 If the problem persists, it may indicate a more serious blockage farther down the pipework. If you're unsure, call a plumber!

To fill or not to fill?

✳ If your toilet tank isn't filling, remove the lid and check that the float ball is securely attached to the float arm, lift wires or chain, and trip lever.

✳ If the tank is filling continuously, you should check that the flush valve is working. If water is constantly running into the tank, you may need to replace a worn tank ball or flapper, which sits over the flush valve.

✳ If water is pouring out through the overflow, check that the float arm is adjusted so that the level of water is below the overflow outlet. Bend it down slightly to lower the water level.

Did you know that...?

...electricity is conducted along cables through, usually, copper wire. The earth beneath our feet is also an efficient conductor of electricity and any that escapes through exposed or unconnected wires will flow toward the ground, taking the shortest route and passing through any object in its way. If you happen to be touching that object, or are the object itself, the consequences can range from a mild shock to serious injury or death.

That's why grounding wire to channel wayward electric current is included in wiring systems. A ground fault won't necessarily cause the circuit to cut out, but ground-fault protection will break the circuit when any leakage passes through an outside conductor.

Grounding-fault protection can be included in the main service panel so that the home's entire electricity supply is protected. Otherwise it can be provided for individual outlets by using receptacles with a ground-fault circuit-interrupter (GFCI).

Blow-out!

Each electrical circuit in the home is connected to a circuit breaker. This has a fuse that blows if there's an electrical fault. Most modern circuit breakers are in the form of a switch that's thrown in the circuit when the fuse blows. When the problem has been identified and dealt with, the switch can be switched back to the "on" position.

Water and electricity don't mix

Water is a very good conductor of electricity and great care should be taken not to mix the two. There are Codes governing the positioning of electrical outlets in bathrooms and kitchens—which is why you have no outlets or switches too near sinks.

✳ Always get a qualified electrician to carry out any work in kitchens and bathrooms.

✳ Don't operate switches with wet hands and keep all appliances at a safe distance from the water source.

✳ Never use an extension cord in a bathroom to plug in appliances such as heaters.

✳ Warning! Don't switch circuits back on (or replace fuses) until the problem has been identified and dealt with. If in doubt, consult an electrician.

Handywoman helpline

Q: I never seem to have enough outlets for all the appliances that I need to plug in. Are there any solutions apart from having to get extra receptacles put in?

A: The number of appliances we use has increased enormously in recent years and few homes have enough outlets. To solve this problem, you can plug a 6-outlet power strip into a receptacle.

Power strips are handy for computers, printers, and lamps, which require relatively low wattage. Outlets, however, shouldn't be abused: it's better to get an electrician to put in extra receptacles than risk overloading the circuit.

Safety first

✳ Make sure the electrical receptacles you are using for your appliances provide the right amperage. General circuits are 15-amp or 20-amp. This is sufficient for most things, but some appliances, such as ranges, require a 40-amp circuit or higher.

✳ When installing a new appliance check the instructions that come with it very carefully. If in doubt, always consult an electrician.

✳ Safety is the top priority with electricity. The best safety precaution is to shut off the circuit breaker or remove the fuse in the main service panel when making even minor repairs to electrical appliances, fixtures, switches, or outlets.

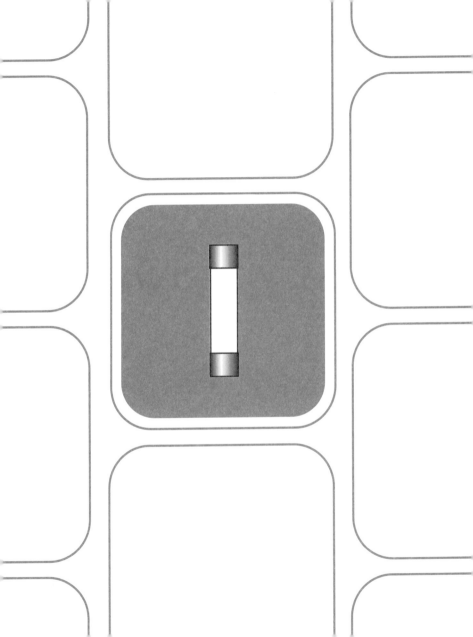

Did you know that...?

…many lighting systems are now low-voltage, operating at 12 or 24 volts. They may need a transformer to reduce the main voltage. When buying a reputable brand, the transformer is normally included, either incorporated in the light fixture itself, in the plug, in a separate plug-in section on the cord, or sometimes in the light bulb. If you need a separate transformer, specifications and instructions on connection will be included.

Computer control

Unless computer and entertainment equipment cables and cords are kept under control they can look unsightly. Hide them away altogether, feed them through specially designed cable covers, or turn them into a feature.

✳ Keep cables organized, labeled if necessary, and accessible.

✳ Keep all wiring safe from accidental disconnection by feet, children, and pets. The simplest way is to gather the wires together and tie them with plastic wire ties, string or even fancy ribbon. Screw cup hooks under a desk or table and loop them up out of sight and out of danger.

✳ Use flexible plastic sleeving through which several cables can be fed for a neat, businesslike look. Alternatively, secure panels to walls, table backs, or desk legs to hide all cables and plugs.

✹ Place televisions and sound systems on lidded boxes or chests. Drill holes so any cables can be fed through and kept inside. Drill holes in shelves or use bracketed shelving systems with gaps at the back.

Power surge

Power surges can occur in our electricity supply, sometimes from faults on our own circuits but also occasionally in the supply from the electricity provider. Computers and other electronic equipment can be sensitive to such surges so it's a good idea to use power strips fitted with a surge suppressor. Alternatively, get an electrician to install a special outlet.

CLEANING

Ten cleaning basics

BROOM: For sweeping floors. Soft bristles will gather the dust as well as the loose dirt, and will poke more easily into corners.

DUSTPAN AND BRUSH: Essential not only for the collection and disposal of sweepings but also a safe way to gather up broken glass or china and nasties such as pet accidents or the occasional dead mouse.

MOP: You can get down on your hands and knees to clean a floor but using a mop is easier. You'll need a wet mop for washing and a dry one for dusting floors.

BUCKET: Everyone needs a bucket. Bright plastic is inexpensive, but chic. Galvanized metal, stainless steel, and white enamel are very designer but also heavy and noisy.

 RAGS AND DUSTERS: Whether you invest in the latest hi-tech duster or just use a torn-up old undershirt, a plentiful selection of clean rags or purchased cleaning cloths is essential.

 SCRUBBING BRUSHES: Sometimes good old-fashioned scrubbing is the only way to get things clean. Choose from bristles in wood or trendy modern plastic.

7 **SCOURERS**: Flat, nylon scourers are good for cleaning pots and pans but are also great for scrubbing off built-up dirt, for example on woodwork in preparation for repainting.

8 **TOOTHBRUSHES**: There are 101 uses for an old toothbrush. Cleaning around faucets, in the corners of window frames, and in the crevices of ornaments are just three.

9 **VACUUM CLEANER**: A vacuum cleaner is the domestic equivalent of a best friend. It's the only really efficient way of removing dust and can be used for everything from floors to furniture.

SPONGES: Available in lots of shapes, sizes, and compositions. Big foam ones are fine for sloshing on lots of suds but not so good at mopping them up. Heavier ones are more absorbent, while small, natural sponges are great for cleaning delicate objects.

Handywoman helpline

Q: I'm bewildered by the range of cleaning products on the market. What do I really need to do the job?

A: Cream cleansers are slightly abrasive but won't damage smooth surfaces. Use on sinks, bathtubs, toiltes, and very grubby or stained worktops, but always consult the label first.

✳ General-purpose floor and wall cleaners are for mopping floors and washing worktops, kitchen surfaces, and paintwork. They're nonabrasive and so are ideal for wiping down stoves and appliances because they dissolve grease as well as dirt.

✳ Window and glass cleaners do what they say. Some contain vinegar, which adds to their cleaning power.

✳ Chlorine bleach kills germs and bleaches. Use for drains, sinks, and toilets and for sterilizing worktops, equipment, and so forth. Use a weak solution for washing down or soaking and a stronger solution, or neat, for bleaching out stains.

✳ Mild soap and detergent are suitable for cleaning delicate surfaces and as a frequent-wash cleaner. Old-fashioned blocks of household soap are mild and relatively free from added chemicals. Eco-friendly brands are also available.

Eight handywoman floor-cleaning tips

1 A vacuum cleaner is the most effective way of removing dust and can be used on all floors (but don't use the beating type of vacuum cleaner on hard or shiny floors as they'll get scratched).

2 Use vacuum cleaner tools to suck up dust around edges and underneath things.

3 Keep a broom, dusting mop, or carpet sweeper handy for crumbs, spills, and things brought in on the soles of shoes.

4 Remove dirt and grease from vinyl, concrete, and ceramic floors with a proprietary floor cleaner.

5 For stone floors, use gentle soap or a specialty cleaner.

6 To prevent smears on shiny floor tiles, dry with an old towel or absorbent cloth.

7 Nonglazed tiles absorb more dirt and may need an occasional scrubbing with a mildly abrasive cleaner. Don't use soap because it will leave a dull film.

8 Clean the grout between floor tiles with detergent or a mildly abrasive cleaner on a brush.

Don't even think about it!

Don't use water on wooden floors, although polyurethane varnish or laminated floor finishes can be mopped or washed using warm water with a few drops of mild detergent and a very well-squeezed-out cloth or mop. For waxed or oiled floors, vacuum or dust frequently using a dusting mop. Only rewax if the floor is dull or very dirty.

Handywoman helpline

Q: I've seen several multipurpose floor-cleaning products that promise protection, stain-resistance, and instant shine. Are they worth the money?

A: Use these products with caution because they often build up over time into a coating that becomes dull, dirty, and worn. And what's more, they're difficult to remove.

Worktop wizard

✳ Worktops should be washed or wiped down frequently using a clean cloth. A solution of bleach will kill germs.

✳ Wooden worktops need occasional re-oiling, but you can dab sunflower oil on dry patches in between.

✳ Never allow lemon juice to come into contact with stone worktops: it burns into the surface.

Shortcuts to stain-removal success

✳ Tea, coffee, red wine, and cola can be removed with soda water. Mop up any excess, pour on soda water, and soak up with clean rags. You shouldn't have to rub, but if you do, always work from the outside in to avoid spreading the stain.

✳ Keep a proprietary spot cleaner handy for difficult stains such as ink or dye; apply immediately and then follow the instructions.

✳ Tackle stains in stainless steel or porcelain sinks with cream cleanser or, if that fails, with a solution of chlorine bleach.

Handywoman tips for cleaning...

...WINDOWS: Use a spray window-cleaner and rub off with clean, lintfree cloths. If very dirty, wash with warm water and detergent first, dry thoroughly, then use the spray.

...PAINTED WALLS: Remove marks using a mild detergent and a sponge or cloth, although this may remove the paint and leave a discolored patch. Repainting is often best.

...LIMESCALE: Use limescale-remover in the toilet and for faucets.

...PLASTIC AND METAL: A duster slightly dampened with a little water or spray cleaner works well.

...UPHOLSTERY: A vacuum cleaner with a good set of attachments works best.

"A vacuum cleaner with a good set of attachments works best for upholstery."

...**WOOD**: Give wood an occasional polish with a good-quality wax polish.

...**FAUCETS**: Use cream toothpaste. Rub on with your fingers and rinse well.

...**SLATTED WINDOW BLINDS**: Clean in the shower or bathtub using the shower attachment, a soft brush and mild detergent.

...**GLASS VASES**: Fill with warm water, drop in a couple of denture-cleaning tablets and allow to soak overnight.

...**MILDEW STAINS**: Clean off walls with a mild solution of bleach.

...**WALLPAPER**: Remove stains and marks by rubbing them gently with a balled up wad of white bread.

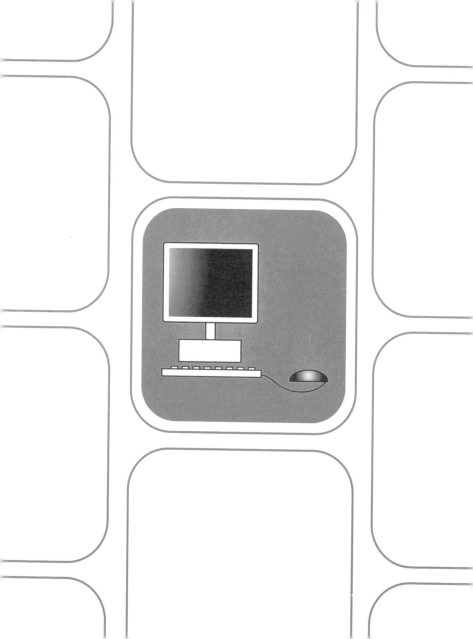

Getting rid of static

Electrical equipment, such as televisions and computers, attract dust via static electricity. Remove frequently with a vacuum cleaner— use the brush attachment on the computer keyboard—or use a duster lightly dampened with an antistatic cleaner.

Computer clean-up

Don't use liquids on computers. Instead, invest in computer screen-cleaning wipes.

I haven't got a thing to wear!

When you're cleaning, you really must dress the part. Gloves—rubber for wet work, fleecy-lined for dusting—are essential for protecting those hands and nails. And why not buy yourself a special cleaning outfit— perhaps a huge printed shirt, a fun headscarf, and a pair of brightly colored, loose-fitting sports pants?

Finally, keep your cleaning materials in a nice box or basket to complement the décor. It will encourage you to use them more often, too.

Handywoman goes eco-friendly

✸ Make your own nonscratch cleanser by mixing ¾ cup of baking soda with ¼ cup of borax and enough dishwashing liquid to form a smooth paste.

✸ Neat white vinegar is good for removing scum and soap buildup in bathtubs and showers. Use diluted to clean windows and mirrors. Will neutralize odors, including pet accidents. Use with baking soda to make foaming cleansers. Because it's acidic, don't use it on porous surfaces such as grouting.

✸ Lemon juice is a natural disinfectant and bleach. Use instead of bleach to remove stains on clothes, worktops, and hands. Be careful and never allow it to come into contact with any form of stone because it burns.

✳ Borax is a general-purpose cleaner that's been around for centuries. Not as corrosive as vinegar or lemon juice.

✳ Baking soda (sodium bicarbonate) has abrasive and deodorizing properties and is brilliant at removing stains. Can be used on clothes, carpets, and wallpaper as well as on stained teapots, vacuum flasks, and casserole dishes. Dissolves grease and mineral deposits and makes a powerful cleanser for sinks when mixed with vinegar.

✳ Keep moths away with cedar wood and lavender rather than with mothballs.

index